England
Resounding

Only through its historical characteristics does music acquire its relation to the unattainable. Without historical mediations, understood as a mere principle or primal phenomenon, it would be utterly impoverished, abstract and in the real sense, lacking in essence.

Consideration of the contemporary relation of philosophy and music leads to the insight that the timeless essence of music must be viewed as a chimera. Only history itself, real history with all its suffering and all its contradiction, constitutes the truth of music.

Theodor W. Adorno, *Essays in Music*

England Keith Alldritt
Resounding

Elgar, Vaughan Williams, Britten and the English Musical Renaissance

ROBERT HALE

First published in 2019 by
Robert Hale, an imprint of
The Crowood Press Ltd,
Ramsbury, Marlborough
Wiltshire SN8 2HR

www.crowood.com

British Library Cataloguing-in-Publication Data
A catalogue record for this book is available from the British Library.

ISBN 978 0 7198 2975 8

Typeset by Chapter One Book Production, Knebworth

Printed and bound in India by Parksons Graphics

For Janet

With love and gratitude for making this book possible

Contents

Acknowledgements

I am grateful for the kind help of Hugh Cobbe and The Vaughan Williams Trust. I must also thank Dr Nick Clark of the Britten Pears Library for his resourceful assistance.

Introduction

IN THIS BOOK I offer an account of the spectacular revival of serious music in England that began at the start of the twentieth century. It was music of a semantic richness that had not been produced in this country since the time of Purcell and Handel. The renaissance was begun by Edward Elgar and sustained, most robustly and protractedly, by composers from the next two generations: Ralph Vaughan Williams and Benjamin Britten. It lasted for at least the first three quarters of the twentieth century and its artefacts were of a quality to equal those created in this same period by the art form traditionally seen as the predominant one in English culture: literature.

Benjamin Britten never met Elgar. Vaughan Williams knew them both – but not well. There was no sense of musical legacy to relate them. Indeed, Britten reacted very strongly, sometimes with violent distaste, against the work of his two elders. Nevertheless there were many features in their chief compositions that make them appear to constitute a tradition, not least the highly developed awareness that each had of English literature and their passionate belief in music as a profound and serious art.

The story I have to tell will be something other than a musicological history. I will seek to place the achievements of these three principal figures of the great revival of English music in a much larger context, one that illuminates their relationships with the other arts, particularly with literature, and with the historical forces that impinged on their lives.

There was, for instance, for all three of these English composers, the fact of America. In 1898, the year in which Elgar initiated England's renaissance with the composing of his *Variations on an Original Theme*, popularly known as the *Enigma Variations*, the United States was in the process of joining, and soon clearly surpassing, Britain as a world power. The opportunities and the money available in America attracted all three composers. They each spent time in the United States and each responded very differently to the higher standard of material living and to the democratic manners that they encountered there. More significantly for their music, they each looked to American authors for the texts of some of their most ambitious compositions. An important source for Elgar's early cantatas was the writings of Henry Wadsworth Longfellow, a highly regarded figure in American literary life towards the end of the nineteenth century. Walt Whitman, who has maintained a more enduring reputation as a poet, provided the words for Vaughan Williams's exhilarating first symphony and for several of his other works. The American poet was one of his great inspirations and admirations throughout his life. Benjamin Britten lived in America in the 1930s. His greatest achievements, unlike those of his two predecessors, were in opera and two of his three operatic masterpieces derive from American texts: *Billy Budd* is based on a novella by Herman Melville and *The Turn of the Screw* on one by Henry James.

The emerging influence of America and its culture is just one of the influences conditioning the English musical revival. Another is the rapid and dramatic political change that marked the seventy-five years or so covered by this book. All three composers were extremely aware, socially and politically. Elgar frequently proclaimed his Toryism and even, at one point in his life, discussed the appropriateness of offering himself as a parliamentary candidate for the Conservative and Unionist Party of which he was such an ardent supporter. Vaughan Williams was anything but a Tory. Often a Labour voter but at heart an Asquithian Liberal, he unfailingly took a definitive position on each of the great political issues of the day. As I have shown in my biography of him, he declared, clearly and unambiguously, his attitude to the Boer War, to the issue of Home Rule in Ireland and to the General Strike of 1926. Political principles also drove him to involve himself in the two world wars of the century to a degree far beyond what was expected of a man of his years. Benjamin Britten was similarly conscious politically. Maturing, while at the Royal College of Music and after, among left-wing film and theatre people and close to the then Marxist poet W.H. Auden, Britten was also, in the 1930s and indeed throughout his life, a pro-active pacifist. Such a moral and political position shows itself very explicitly in his *War Requiem*. But Britten's views also show themselves implicitly and more subtly in many other of his works. The greatest works of Elgar and Vaughan Williams are also very much a music of philosophical attitude. In some very obvious respects they are a response to history. Within them there is a long-term movement from one musical genre to another. It proceeds from the choral forms of Elgar's early years, cantatas and oratorios, to the symphony, and thence, in Britten's maturity, to the opera. To take the major works in the chronological order of their composition, as I will do here, is an illuminating way of reading the history of the time and the responses of three unusually perceptive men to it. Other composers such as Gustav Holst, William Walton, Arnold Bax and Malcolm Arnold contributed significantly to the English musical renaissance of this period. But the three who are my subject maintained the most sustained and deepest engagement with the issues presented by the times. As we proceed through the near three quarters of a century I shall have cause to mention the insights offered by the other arts, by poetry, fiction, painting and sculpture. But the main focus will be on the music of these three generations of composers and on the insights and perceptions into the dramas, tragedies and calamities of the century that the semantics of music uniquely convey.

1

Edward Elgar

THE PRECISE MOMENT of the beginning of the radical revival of English music at the end of the nineteenth century has been vividly described by the composer who launched it, Edward Elgar. It happened on the evening of 21 October 1898. The year before, Queen Victoria had celebrated her sixtieth year on the throne of Britain and its worldwide Empire. And just a month before that historic moment for English music there occurred, in the Sudan, the great Battle of Omdurman. It was one of the worst acts of slaughter in the history of the British Empire. An army under General Kitchener, which was amply equipped with Maxim guns and up-to-date artillery, massacred an army of Dervishes who had only pre-industrial weapons. The British offensive was an attempt to reassert imperial power in the region. It was also viewed as an act of revenge for the killing some thirteen years before nearby at Khartoum of General Gordon, who had a reputation in Britain as a heroic, near saintly Christian imperialist. (In 1899 Elgar's proposal for a 'Gordon' symphony was accepted for the Three Choirs Festival in Worcester.) But the avenging of General Gordon at Omdurman with relentless, mechanical slaughter gave pause even to the young Winston Churchill, present as a war journalist and long hardened to the realities of modern warfare. Walking the battlefield two days after the engagement, he was appalled by the sight and stench of the thousands of Dervish dead. They were, he concluded 'destroyed not conquered by machinery'.[1]

This was also the year in which the disgraced Oscar Wilde published his lengthy poem of punishment, humiliation and suffering, *The Ballad of*

Reading Gaol. At the same time his fellow Irishman George Bernard Shaw had a major success with his play *Arms and the Man*, which had for its central theme the futility of war. Another great success during these months was *Hiawatha's Wedding Feast,* a setting by the twenty-three-year-old Samuel Coleridge-Taylor of a text by the then widely admired poet, Henry Wadsworth Longfellow.

But for the forty-one-year old Edward Elgar, then living in suburban Malvern in Worcestershire, there had not yet been any comparable success. He too had composed cantatas using texts by Longfellow: *The Black Knight* of 1892 and *Scenes from the Saga of King Olaf,* first given a performance some five years later. Longfellow was in some respects the Walt Disney of the nineteenth century. Early Disney films such as *The Sword and the Rose* (1953) and *The Story of Robin Hood and his Merrie Men* (1952) are highly reminiscent of the extremely romanticized, emphatically picturesque view of old Europe that Longfellow supplied to his fellow Americans in a novel such as *Hyperion* (1839). And not only Americans. Longfellow was widely read in England. Elgar's mother was a keen admirer. Her son grew up sharing this enthusiasm and it must certainly have helped confirm his delight in the world of feudalism and chivalry. An early expression of this was his concert overture *Froissart* (1890), named for the fourteenth-century French chronicler. Elgar also set *Rondel* (1894), a poem deriving from Froissart and translated into English by Longfellow.

However, none of Elgar's Longfellow settings brought him great success – certainly not financially. He still earned much of his living as an itinerant, overworked musician and music teacher. On the historic evening of 21 October 1898 he was weary after spending much of the day giving violin lessons at The Mount, a girls' school in Malvern. He came home dispirited. Years later he gave an account of what suddenly happened:

> I came home very tired. Dinner being over my dear wife said to me 'Edward, you look like a good cigar', and having lighted it I sat down at the piano …
>
> In a little while, soothed and feeling rested I began to play, and suddenly my wife interrupted by saying: 'Edward that's a good tune'. I awoke from the dream: 'Eh! tune, what tune?' And she said, 'Play it again, I like that tune'. I played and strummed and played, and then she exclaimed: 'That's the tune.'[2]

He played on he remembered, and then

> The voice of C.A.E. [Alice Elgar] asked with a sound of approval, 'What is that?' I answered, 'Nothing – but something might be made of it'.

This was the origin of the work that was to be entitled *Variations on an Original Theme* and is now usually referred to as the *Enigma Variations*. It was Elgar's breakthrough work and vastly enhanced his reputation in Britain, and within a few years successful performances in Germany and Russia helped to bring him European fame.

For all its Worcestershire associations, audiences abroad will have enjoyed the work simply as music, for the impressive sequences of sound it contains, with all its many changes in texture, speed, tone and volume, with its alternations from the skittish to the noble, from the knockabout to the near sacred. Distant audiences will probably not have taken a great deal of interest in the piece as the kind of programme music that Elgar indicated in his dedication of the work 'to my friends pictured within'. But programmatic the work certainly is in one important respect and writers on Elgar have offered a great deal of background information and characterizations of the fourteen individuals, nine men and five women, evoked for us in the music. Looked at in this way the *Enigma Variations* is a sound picture of life in a rural English county at the very end of Queen Victoria's long reign. With its wide range of characters, mostly middle class and cultured, and one of them titled, it recalls the group portrait created by George Eliot in her great novel *Middlemarch*, published almost a quarter of a century before the *Enigma Variations*. This too gives us a vivid sense of a small town and a rural community at the very end of a readily definable historical period, at a moment of historical change.

Elgar's *Variations* do not, of course, probe the failings, limitations and suffering in provincial life that George Eliot investigates. The group portrait of Elgar's circle of Worcestershire and Malvern friends is for the most part a sunny one, showing the individuals 'pictured within' as amusing, entertaining, sensitive, good-hearted. Some of them are people of emotional and spiritual depths.

But the well-to-do country town of Malvern, where he lived from 1891 to 1899, was but one half of Elgar's story over the years as he struggled and persevered to establish himself as a composer. The other half was Birmingham.

In 1882, the year that Wagner's final opera *Parsifal* had its debut at the

Festspielhaus in Bayreuth, the twenty-five-year old Edward Elgar took a lowly musical job in Birmingham. He was engaged to play among the second violins in William Stockley's Orchestra. This was Birmingham's very first symphony orchestra and had been established in the fast-thriving industrial city just over a quarter of a century before Elgar joined as a very junior member. He would work for Stockley for some seven years, that is to say until he was thirty-two and had a wife who was able to help support him financially.

The job in Birmingham provided a significant part of his income as a young jobbing musician. Verdi once spoke of his 'years in the galleys' as an aspiring opera composer. Elgar's seven years as an obscure orchestral player constitute a similar protracted period of struggle. For seven years, a span of time with a biblical ring to it, Elgar commuted regularly between the country quiet of the small cathedral city of Worcester and the din, dirt and smells of Britain's greatest centre of heavy industry and manufacturing. His train would take him from Worcester through the green, well-wooded, orchard countryside of his native county into and along the southern fringe of the Black Country, and thence to the vast, noisy railway station in Birmingham with its reek of coal and hiss of thronging steam trains. For seven years he would make his way up either Colmore Row or New Street. In Elgar's time New Street was far grander than it is today. It was lined with imposing banks, stylish shops, department stores and arcades that were patronized by elegantly dressed members of the city's moneyed middle class. (A mosaic at the entrance to the city's art gallery commemorates the urbanity of Corporation Street at that time.) As Elgar, the struggling country musician, moved up the incline of the grand thoroughfare there would come into sight the Town Hall, the dramatic and characterful Birmingham landmark that stood, and stands, as an important site in the history of English music. It would be the scene of memorable occasions in Elgar's career long after he left what he knew as 'Mr Stockley's Orchestra'. To his right as he approached the top of the rise that is New Street Elgar would have seen Christchurch, an early nineteenth-century church in the Classical style but endowed with a spire. It stood between the columned Town Hall and the newly built Council House. This latter building was a much larger, grander place with a busy baroque frontage and a soaring cupola. A showy construction, it had been completed and opened just three years before Elgar began working for William Stockley and was ostentatious testimony to the new wealth of Birmingham at the time. The older and more modest Christchurch was important for Birmingham people because, unlike other Anglican churches, it did not charge to rent a pew. It was also reputed to contain the remains of one of Birmingham's many famous eighteenth-century entrepreneurs, the printer and type designer John Baskerville. In the year in which the *Enigma Variations* was first performed, this beloved church at the very centre of the city was pulled down and replaced by luxury shops.

The nearby Town Hall to which, for seven years, Elgar regularly directed his steps was closely involved with the musical life of Birmingham. Indeed it had been built to cater to it. One of England's great provincial occasions for the performance of serious music had long been the Birmingham Triennial Festival. It had been founded in 1784 and became an important part of Birmingham's burgeoning intellectual life. Some fifty years earlier the young Samuel Johnson had lived in the city for four years, lodging for a time in the High Street in the house of Thomas Warren, the founder of the city's first newspaper, the *Birmingham Journal*. The venture was a precursor of the intellectual ferment at the end of the eighteenth century that led to the achievements of the Lunar Society, which met locally and in the city. It was these achievements that provided much of the theoretical as well as practical expertise that made Birmingham the fountainhead of the Industrial Revolution.

The rapid expansion of the city that came from industrialization created a large working class in the city, many of which came from Ireland and were Roman Catholic. One of the reasons that Cardinal John Henry Newman founded the Birmingham Oratory in 1847 was to cater for the spiritual needs of this transplanted community. This was the same year in which Karl Marx, Friedrich Engels and others offered those in the exploited working class an alternative view of salvation with the founding in London of the Communist League.

Newman was a prominent figure in the intense theological and ecclesiastical turbulence of the nineteenth century. He was a leading member of the Oxford Movement, arguing for the introduction of more Catholic elements into the Church of England. Beginning his career as an Anglican priest, this extremely gifted apologist converted to Roman Catholicism in 1845, thereby bringing a moment of drama and shock into English church history. In Rome Newman was authorized by Pope Pius IX to establish a religious community in England. Newman came to industrial Birmingham. He first gathered his followers together in an old gin distillery in Deritend, the medieval quarter of the city that by then had become something of a slum. He next proceeded to found his Oratory at St Anne's, Alcester Street, a Gothic Revival building he had built nearby in the Digbeth area of central Birmingham. The community later moved to a more pleasant area in Hagley Road, Edgbaston, where another church was erected in 1852. Newman dedicated his Oratory church to the sixteenth-century Italian priest St Philip Neri, who founded an oratory in Rome where he ministered to the sick and poor. One of the devotional aids he employed in services was the use of *laude spirituale* or sacred songs. In time these became more complex and were known as oratorios; among St Philip's followers who composed music for services there was Palestrina. The Newman Oratory on the southwest side of Birmingham thus related to a distinguished strain in the history of the cultural context of Catholic religious practice. The institution became a well-known feature of Birmingham life from the late nineteenth century onwards, often referred to locally as 'Little Rome in Brum'. Like the grand landmark Town Hall and the Triennial Festival, the Birmingham Oratory was to play an important part in the life of the composer of *The Dream of Gerontius*.

Founded in 1783, the year that saw the conclusion of the American War of Independence, the Birmingham Triennial Festival grew rapidly and acquired an ever-expanding audience in the city and in its environs. The Festival was originally held in St Philip's, a Baroque church (now a cathedral) built in 1715 by Thomas Archer, the architect of St John's, Smith Square, in London. This church was part of the westward expansion of the city from its medieval centre around St Martin's in the Bull Ring. Showing the influence of Borromini, whose buildings Archer had seen in Rome, St Philip's, like many English churches of the period, had extensive wooden galleries to accommodate a larger congregation than would have been possible in a medieval church with a comparably sized ground plan. Despite this the church became too small as audiences grew and the Triennial Festival transferred to the Theatre Royal on New Street. By the early nineteenth century such was the size of the audience for serious music that this venue again proved too small and the idea of a purpose-built hall for the Festival was proposed. Such were the origins of Birmingham Town Hall, which lay more in the musical than in the political life of the city. This was in 1832, the year of the eventual passing of the Great Reform Bill and in which George Eliot set her novel *Middlemarch*, where the dramatic political struggle for the extension of voting rights provides a shadowy but highly significant background.

The imposing concert venue that is Birmingham Town Hall was an

architectural expression of the civic self-consciousness and confidence
that the Industrial Revolution and its attendant wealth brought to the city.
It was this confidence, here and in the other burgeoning industrial cities,
that compelled the political recognition and representation granted by the
Great Reform Bill of 1832. Birmingham Town Hall was first planned in that
same year and was completed and opened two years later. Still outstanding
amidst modern high-rise Birmingham, the building is a Corinthian temple
in the robust Roman style that emerged in British public buildings in the
early nineteenth century. The sequence of emphatic columns that enclose the
outer walls, inspired by the proportions of the Temple of Castor and Pollux
in the Roman Forum, allude to its origins in the Roman Republic, which
was a political model attractive to the energetic radicals of Birmingham and
other fast-developing cities at the time of the Reform Bill.

After its opening the Town Hall soon attracted such leading figures in
nineteenth-century musical life as Mendelssohn and Saint-Saëns. It was also
the most important location in Edward Elgar's long and arduous progress from
obscurity as an impecunious violinist, travelling up from the country to a
lowly place among the second violins in 'Mr Stockley's Orchestra' at the Town
Hall, to sudden, brilliant celebrity. Some twenty years later in 1903, the year in
which King Edward VII was proclaimed Emperor of India, Elgar was the star
at one of the grandest social and musical occasions ever seen in Birmingham
Town Hall. This was the first performance of his oratorio *The Apostles*. Having
achieved success with works such as the *Enigma Variations*, *The Dream of
Gerontius* and the Military March no. 1 ('Pomp and Circumstance'), Elgar
now entered the Town Hall as an acclaimed celebrity. The demand for tickets
to the premiere was such that extra seating had been installed. A large crowd
stood outside the Town Hall to watch distinguished members of the audience
arrive. Earl Howe, a prominent Conservative politician and President of the
Triennial Festival, arrived with his wife. They were soon followed by members
of Birmingham's dynastic family, the Chamberlains of Highbury Hall in
Moseley, the ladies strikingly dressed. The *Birmingham Daily Mail* reported,

> A large party came from Highbury, Mrs Chamberlain who was wearing a
> red costume with black hat, being accompanied by the Misses Chamberlain
> and several other ladies and Mr Neville Chamberlain ... so fashionable was
> the assembly this morning that comparatively few of the visitors arrived on
> foot ... When Dr Elgar took his seat shortly before half-past eleven every

inch of the interior of the vast building was occupied by an audience which will undoubtedly rank as one of the most brilliant of the many distinguished companies seen within the walls of the historic hall.[3]

Elgar's slow, difficult rise to such eminence was very much in and through Birmingham. As a young man avid and energetic in the pursuit of recognition as a composer he had attempted many forays into the musical world of London. And indeed he had enjoyed some successes at the concerts organized and conducted at the Crystal Palace by Sir August Manns, which were an important part of the musical offerings in the capital from 1855 to 1901. But up to the time of Elgar's marriage in October 1889, and to a lesser extent afterwards, Birmingham was an indispensable source of income and opportunities for performing his compositions.

William Stockley's memoir of musical life in Birmingham contains kindly recollections of the young Elgar and also conveys the intense energy that pervaded the musical life of the city and the nearby Black Country at the time. His book shows very clearly how there was a vital, fast-growing musical culture in provincial England long before there were any renowned English composers. Elgar, Vaughan Williams and Britten were later to have careers that were only possible with these foundations. Stockley's musical zeal could be, in more than one sense of the word, messianic. Here is his account of one of his numerous idealistic musical ventures:

> It occurred to me that there was one class in town to which the enjoyment of music was almost impossible, through the nature of their occupation, viz., cabmen and drivers and conductors of omnibuses. Their loss was the harder, inasmuch as they conveyed others to the concerts etc., which they themselves had no chance of attending. I therefore laid the matter before the band and chorus and they cheerfully agreed to give up Sunday afternoon for a really good concert if the Town Hall could be secured for the purpose.
>
> The Mayor readily consented to give us the hall for free if we would perform sacred music and make the concert a kind of service. This we, of course, did, the Mayor giving a short address and the whole company joining in the Old Hundredth Psalm.
>
> The Town Hall Mission kindly helped by conveying the invitations and a unique audience of cabmen etc. and their families assembled in goodly numbers to hear a selection from *The Messiah*.[4]

In 1883, when Elgar was twenty-six and in his first year of commuting to Birmingham, he was excited to report to a friend that his *Sérénade mauresque* had been accepted by Stockley for a performance at Birmingham Town Hall. It is a pleasing piece catering to the taste for the Moorish that so strongly affected late Victorian design and is conspicuously on display in Leighton House in Kensington. It was also a feature of the Alhambra Court, which was added as part of the reconstruction of the Crystal Palace at Sydenham, south London, in 1854. Alhambras proliferated throughout the country and the vogue for North African exoticism would reach the height of its popularity with Rudolph Valentino as *The Sheik* (1921) and Sigmund Romberg's operetta *The Desert Song* (1926). The *Sérénade mauresque* is more muted, showing us an Elgar in the kasbah enjoying some local colour but innocent of anything sounding like belly dancing. The piece was well received at the Town Hall. 'I had a good success at Birm. Despite what the papers say',[5] he told his friend, the cellist and doctor Charles Buck. The slighting review, he explained, had been by a fellow composer who boasted a degree in music, but whose composition had proved unplayable at the concert.

On occasion Elgar himself submitted work to Stockley that the conductor rejected as unperformable. At the beginning of 1886 he told Dr Buck about a Scottish overture that is now lost. 'Oh: about the Scottish overture ... I showed it to old Stockley and he candidly said he could not read the Score (*sic*) and it sounded to him disconnected.' Elgar was evidently much discouraged by the rejection and announced a moderating of his ambitions as a composer: 'So I have retired into my shell and live in hopes of writing a polka someday – failing that a single chant is probably my fate.'[6]

But early in 1889, the year in which he composed the charming piano piece *Salut d'amour*, which made a good deal of money for its publisher Schott, Elgar's relationship with the Stockley Concert Orchestra improved markedly. He was invited to take to the rostrum and conduct his latest composition, an orchestral suite. (Michael Kennedy has suggested that this was 'probably' the work which after revision became the Serenade in E minor, Elgar's opus 1.) Elgar was extremely proud of his new standing as a conductor and of the performance he gave in January 1888 when he was thirty. And this in spite of, again, some negative reviewing. He told Dr Buck, 'I had a good success in Birmingham with my Suite, but the critics, save two, are nettled. I am the only local man who has been asked to conduct his own work – and what is a greater offence, I *did* it – and *well* too; for this I must needs suffer.'[7]

The following year Elgar was married. He now left Birmingham and the West Midlands behind him. With the moral and financial support of his reasonably well-to-do wife, Alice, he moved to London, settling in Kensington, thereby putting himself in an easier position to make himself known in the capital city, the centre of the musical culture of the nation. But the venture finally proved unsuccessful and in less than two years the couple returned to Worcestershire. They rented a house, Forli, in suburban Malvern and Elgar again advertised his services as a violin teacher.

Compositionally, however, the years in London were by no means a failure. A work from that time that still enjoys performances is the concert overture *Froissart*. In her diary Alice Elgar referred to this celebration of the chivalric as a 'tale'. And in many of his longer compositions there is a clear narrative element, despite his repudiation of the programmatic in music later in life on a great public occasion in Birmingham. Alice was unable to attend the first performance at the Shire Hall in Worcester of his evocation of medieval noblesse; it was the time of the birth of the couple's daughter Carice. Some four months later, however, she was extremely proud when she went to Birmingham Town Hall to hear her husband's salute to the famous chronicler of the Middle Ages. A new and exciting level of achievement in this familiar venue was reached when Elgar was summoned to the platform to acknowledge the enthusiastic applause of the Birmingham audience.

As he persevered in promoting his career as a composer from his base in Malvern, for a period in the 1890s Birmingham ceased to be the regular looked-to source of income that it had been in his middle years. Assiduously he worked at getting his compositions performed all over the country. His cantata *Caractacus* had its first performance at the Leeds Festival in 1898. Another cantata, *Scenes from the Saga of King Olaf*, premiered at the Potteries town of Hanley at the North Staffordshire Musical Festival. The Serenade in E minor was first played at the then fashionable seaside resort (complete with tower) of New Brighton on Merseyside.

He also, at a distance from the capital, resumed the struggle to make his work known and recognized in London. The light but successful pieces *Chanson de matin* and *Chanson de nuit* were first played at the Queen's Hall in Langham Place, which was just beginning to compete with St James's Hall in Piccadilly as the premier concert venue in central London. His *Imperial March* was first played at the Crystal Palace conducted by the eminent impresario and conductor August Manns. And at last in June 1899 came the breakthrough occasion with the first performance of the *Enigma Variations* at the venerable St James's Hall. The venue stood at the very heart of the imperial capital, fronting on to Piccadilly on one side and Regent Street on the other. The grand interior was decorated in an eclectic Victorian style reminiscent of both the Italian Renaissance and, again, the Moorish Alhambra palace in Granada. Little wonder that, with his ability to obtain performances in such a venue, Birmingham became less important to his career.

Even by 1897, following the first performance of *King Olaf*, Elgar was coming to regard Birmingham as but one of a number of cities in a queue to stage his compositions: Liverpool, Bradford, Birmingham and Wolverhampton. 'They follow of course on the C. Palace – like sheep – but alas! For us musicians there are so few pioneers ... who will stand up and say "this thing is worthy" ...'[8] But in the autumn of 1898 Birmingham did a little better. The committee of the Triennial Festival proposed that half a concert be devoted to his works. Elgar, conscious of his improving standing in the larger music world, agreed, though underwhelmed and grudgingly. He told the *Daily Telegraph* music critic Joseph Bennett, 'I received an official request from Birmingham ... but they offer a ½ programme ... I *think* I ought to have a whole programme now.'[9]

Within a year, however, Birmingham had come back with a far better proposal: the organizers of the city's Triennial Festival offered him a commission 'to write a large work'. The result was to be a milestone in Elgar's career and in the history of English music. The work that Elgar delivered and that was first performed in the Town Hall in the first year of the new century, with William Stockley conducting, was *The Dream of Gerontius*.

Today this work is recognized as the supreme achievement among Elgar's many works of choral music. But the process of its composition was difficult, even painful and its first public performance was for Elgar a catastrophe and a moment of deep despair. His first idea for the Birmingham commission was an oratorio on the subject of the conversion of Britain to Christianity by St Augustine of Canterbury. A few years earlier he had toyed with setting the *Civitas Dei*, a text by the Church Father who shared the name, St Augustine of Hippo. This was a subject that he would consider again in later years and one that was to provide a revealing link between him and Vaughan Williams.

But now as he considered possibilities for the Birmingham Triennial Festival, the subject of the saint who had led the Gregorian mission to bring Roman Catholicism to Britain, already in part subscribing to Celtic

Christianity, posed problems. England at the turn of the twentieth century was a society in which theological and sectarian issues had a vastly greater social and political importance than they do today. Elgar's devout and erudite Catholicism was often a disadvantage to him in advancing his career: in January 1899 he had to report to a journalist friend that his proposal of St Augustine of Canterbury as a subject had been rejected by the organizing committee of the Triennial Festival as 'too controversial; this is as I feared.'[10]

So, paradoxically, Elgar turned to *The Dream of Gerontius*, a poem by the most divisive and controversial theologian of Victorian England, Cardinal John Henry Newman. At the Three Choirs Festival of September 1899 Elgar had a long walk with Father Bellamy of the Birmingham Oratory, who had known Newman personally and was a jealous and protective admirer of his famous poem. But Elgar's publisher at Novello & Co., Alfred Littleton, was sceptical about the project. Elgar was greatly discouraged and reached the point of thinking of abandoning the commission, but the chairman of the Birmingham Triennial Festival committee hastened to Malvern to reassure him. This was George Hope Johnstone, who was Birmingham through and through. Born in Handsworth, he had pursued his highly successful career in the city's jewellery quarter. The highly profitable firm he created specialized in cufflinks, waistcoat buttons and collar studs. On New Year's Day 1900, after they had gone to church together, Johnstone guaranteed his support to his fellow Catholic and offered much better terms for the commission. Twelve days later Elgar visited Father Neville, Newman's executor and friend, at the Oratory. With the priest's authorization and encouragement he devoted himself single-mindedly to the work during the spring of 1900 and completed it in the first week of June. It was, he told his close friend August Jaeger, 'awfully solemn and mystic'.[11]

Four months later *The Dream of Gerontius* had its first performance at Birmingham Town Hall on 30 October 1900. The country was involved in a general election, which, surely to Elgar's delight, resulted in a Conservative majority for the Prime Minister Lord Salisbury. But the first performance of his oratorio, rooted as it was in his deepest beliefs and feelings, brought him only disappointment and distress.

The premiere of *The Dream of Gerontius* was one of the great disasters in musical history. A leading cause was the sudden death, at the very moment that rehearsals were getting under way, of the chorus master Charles Swinnerton Heap. Yet another Brummie, born ten years before Elgar, this keen promoter of Elgar's music had begun his musical career as a boy soprano singing with William Stockley's orchestra at the Birmingham Triennial Festival. He later studied at Leipzig and St John's College, Cambridge, and went on to teach at the newly founded Royal College of Music. He was an understanding and enthusiastic supporter of Elgar during the younger man's years of struggle, and succeeded in obtaining for him the commission for *King Olaf* for the North Staffordshire Musical Festival at Hanley. Elgar long remembered his debt to Heap and dedicated two compositions to him: the oratorio *The Light of Life* and the Organ Sonata in G major (1895) with its extremely challenging finale. Elgar later commented that without Heap's support he would have 'remained in outer darkness'.

The unexpected death of his fellow Midlander and supporter, just as choral preparations for *Gerontius* were beginning, was a doubly grievous blow, for Heap understood Elgar's music as many contemporaries did not, and rehearsed it with sympathetic insight and belief. It was also an incalculable loss for the *Gerontius* premiere that a new chorus master had to be found at minimal notice. Almost the only choice was Elgar's old employer of some twenty years before, William Stockley. The former conductor of the Birmingham Festival Choral Society was now seventy years old and had been in retirement for three years. Rehearsals quickly proved that he now lacked the energy and commitment necessary to inspire the singers into an appreciation of Elgar's score. Furthermore, Stockley had grown up as a Non-conformist and had little sympathy with the Roman Catholic concepts recurring in Cardinal Newman's poem about the journey of a human soul from the moment of death to arrival on the hither shore of Purgatory.

The first performance was to be conducted by Hans Richter, the distinguished associate of Wagner and Brahms and the conductor at the highly successful premiere of the *Enigma Variations*. At the first rehearsal he was greatly dismayed by the inadequacy of the choir's preparation. Wishing to motivate the singers and perhaps uncertain of his powers of eloquence in English, Richter invited Elgar to address the singers. Elgar did so, but not at all tactfully. He came close to losing his temper and told them that they made his music sound little more or better than 'a drawing room ballad'. This telling off of the choir in front of the orchestral players provoked mutterings and resentment. Richter desperately insisted on extra rehearsal time. But to no avail: on the occasion of the first performance the choir was sometimes ragged, sometimes flat.[12]

Elgar's disappointment brought him close to despair. Devout that he was, he concluded that the failure of *Gerontius* was divinely intended and that there was nothing to do but submit to God's will, as he wrote to his close friend and musical adviser August Jaeger:

> I have worked hard for forty years and at the last, Providence denies me a decent hearing of my work: so I submit – I always said God was against art and I still believe it. Anything obscene or trivial is blessed in this world and has a reward – I ask for no reward – only to live and to hear my work. I still hear it in my heart and in my head so I must be content.

The reviews of that first performance of *Gerontius* proved generally to be more favourable than Elgar might have expected. And so too were the recorded comments of many of those present in the Town Hall that day, but not everyone: Ralph Vaughan Williams had enthusiastically travelled to Birmingham expecting to hear a work that would equal the *Enigma Variations*, but he was 'bitterly disappointed' with *Gerontius*. For him it was not just the choir that was unsatisfactory. If Harry Plunket Greene, the bass baritone who sang the role of the Angel of the Agony, had 'lost his voice' then Marie Brema, singing the Guardian Angel, 'had none to lose'. Vaughan Williams's mockery continued: Edward Lloyd sang the title role 'like a Stainer anthem, in the correct tenor attitude with one foot slightly withdrawn'.[13]

But other audience members that day could hear the great achievement and quality in the score underlying the questionable performance. As Jane Stanford, the wife of Charles Villiers Stanford, left the Town Hall in the company of Vaughan Williams she exclaimed to her husband's former pupil, 'Is not that a fine work!'[14] The wife of William Baker, who was referred to in the fourth of the *Enigma Variations* ('W.M.B.'), expressed a similar opinion to Dora Penny, alluded to in the tenth ('Dorabella'): 'A very poor performance but what a wonderful work!' Subsequent performances and the developing reputation of *Gerontius* have long since confirmed its standing as one of the pre-eminent works of English choral music. From the outset the Prelude evokes a sounding of spirituality such as had rarely been heard before in the music of this country. The muted violas, clarinets and bassoons joined by the cor anglais transport the listener swiftly into a very particular world of hushed spirituality. *The Dream of Gerontius* was first heard at a time when the exploration of the spiritual was a central preoccupation in the arts in the West. Stéphane Mallarmé and the French and European symbolists who followed on from him saw it as their task to render 'états d'âme' (states of soul).[15] This is a major concern in the work of the Irish poet W.B. Yeats at this period, especially in his Rose and Rosicrucian poems. The same is also true of the highly wrought poetry of the Russian symbolists at the other end of Europe: Andrei Bely and Alexander Blok.

The Dream of Gerontius of 1900 is very much of this period but it operates within greater dimensions than other works of the time. Its length and its mix of verbal and musical intricacy allow a detailed realization of the states of a human soul as it reaches and then transcends the ending of its mortality. It is a rich and powerful mingling of choral and orchestral writing. Different states and textures of spiritual experience are dwelled on. But there are also dramatic musical interventions punctuating and sectioning the progress of the narrative. There is the disconcerting entry of the snarling demons, the stirring hymn tune that emerges as Gerontius approaches the threshold of the afterlife and subsequently the sudden sobering insistences of the Angel of the Agony. And then, at the last, the touching moment when the Guardian Angel bids Gerontius farewell:

Farewell but not for ever! Brother dear,
Be brave and patient on thy bed of sorrow;
Swiftly shall pass thy night of trial here,
And I will come and wake thee on the morrow.

Vaughan Williams's greatest choral work, *Sancta Civitas*, offers an interesting contrast to this in that it ends with a similarly affecting conclusion, not as here with the music of departure but, as we will note later, with the brisk music of divine arrival.

Michael Kennedy was surely right to see a strongly autobiographical component in *The Dream of Gerontius*:

Not only did Elgar bring Newman's poem to life and give expression to his religious beliefs at that time; he expressed unforgettably the darker side of his own nature; the 'sense of ruin' pervades the music, and in Gerontius's anguished cries on his bed of pain can be recognised the tormented spirit discernible in Elgar's letters to Jaeger. From his deepest experience, Elgar created the last great artistic monument of the reign of Queen Victoria and the last of the nineteenth century.[16]

In one of the many letters of this time in which he sought to write of the autobiographical basis of the work, Elgar apologizes for 'pleonasm' or verbal excess in his attempt to speak of *Gerontius* in terms of his own life close to the Malvern Hills.

> I think you will find Gerontius (*sic*) far beyond anything I've yet done – I like it – I am not suggesting that I have risen to the heights of the poem for one moment – but on our hillside night after night looking across the 'illimitable' horizon (pleonasm!) I've seen in thought the Soul go up and have written my own heart's blood into the score.
>
> You must hear it in Birmingham.[17]

There was always a conflict in Elgar between his lyric drive to express himself from 'his own heart's blood' and his desire to give a broader account of experience. For all the autobiographical, lyrical influences that lay behind Elgar's finest works, he struggled resolutely during the first years of his career, based in the Midlands, to compose more impersonal works of heroic narrative, such as *Caractacus* and *King Olaf*. With the influence of Wagner so powerful and pervasive at the time, it is understandable that an aspiration to epic is discernible in those musical narratives. In his book *The Epic Strain in the English Novel* E.M.W. Tillyard, clearly itemizing the components of epic, identified its influence and presence in some of the great fiction of the late nineteenth century and the early twentieth, for example in George Eliot's *Middlemarch* and in Joseph Conrad's *Nostromo*. It is even more conspicuously there in D.H. Lawrence's *The Rainbow* and its sequel *Women in Love*, which is full of Wagnerian allusions. Both novels were published within Elgar's lifetime. So too were the early parts of the *Cantos* by Ezra Pound, which also offer a heroic vision of the history of civilization.

The epic aspirations of the time very much inspire and infuse the next two works that Elgar was to compose for the Birmingham Triennial Festival. The first was *The Apostles* which had its premiere at a grand social occasion in Birmingham Town Hall in October 1903. Elgar had long been considering the epic story of the life of Jesus. He wrote his own text after a great deal of research into biblical sources and consulting both Henry Wadsworth

Longfellow's version of the Christian story, *The Divine Tragedy* (1871), and Richard Wagner's *Jesus von Nazareth: Ein dichterischer Entwurf* (1848), a sketch of the last weeks in the life of Christ that Wagner drafted as a preliminary text in the composing of an opera that was not to be completed.

The text that Elgar created presents the heroic narrative in seven episodes divided into two parts. The first episode tells of the establishment of the very first Christian community with Christ's calling of the disciples; the second is about Jesus preaching the Gospel; and the third, 'By the Sea of Galilee', perhaps surprisingly, deals with the conversion of Mary Magdalene. In epic fashion, the central story of the hero is contextualized within a group of other carefully realized characters. The foregrounding of Mary Magdalene was something Elgar took from Longfellow. The second part of *The Apostles* again proceeds to widen the context with a gripping characterization of Judas Iscariot and a pondering of his motives. There follows 'Golgotha', an oblique orchestral intimation of the Crucifixion. Then comes the beautiful gentle music of 'At the Sepulchre', followed by a finale in which great, recurring alleluias are sounded forth by the whole ensemble of soloists, chorus and orchestra.

On many occasions in *The Apostles* the music that accompanies and serves to vivify the episodes is moving and memorable. The Prelude is powerful, as is the opening chorus. This is followed by the particularly affecting scene of the coming of the dawn with the notes of the shofar dramatically pervading the music as the disciples, one by one, are summoned. But for all its many fine effects *The Apostles* has not enjoyed the enduring popularity and performance life of *The Dream of Gerontius*. Like many modernist works of literature, painting and music, *The Apostles* is a work of collocation rather than of continuity. But unlike, say, *The Waste Land* or *The Rake's Progress* it lacks a supervening musical design. It sounds more like a series of fragments than an organized and compellingly developed entity.

The work originated, of course, as but a section of a larger work. This is what Elgar sought to develop in the sequel to *The Apostles* which was *The Kingdom*, a work based chiefly on episodes from the Acts of the Apostles. It was a commission from the Birmingham Festival of 1906.

Before this, however, came an involvement with Birmingham of a completely different kind. This was Elgar's acceptance of a professorship of music at the very recently created University of Birmingham. He delivered his inaugural lecture on 16 March 1905.

The Chair, funded by Richard Peyton, was endowed in his name. One of the many enlightened and cultured Birmingham businessmen of the day. Peyton was a member of a family firm of chemical manufacturers, a donor to the new Birmingham Art Gallery and for many years he was an honorary and very energetic officer of the Birmingham Triennial Festival. He often travelled to the continent to recruit artists, including Liszt and Saint-Saëns, to perform in the city. It would appear that the idea of the Elgar appointment was suggested to Peyton by Sir Oliver Lodge, the renowned physicist who served as the first principal of Birmingham University. The possibility of a professorship is said to have originated in a conversation between Lodge and another keen admirer of the composer, Hermann Fiedler, professor of German at the University. Some ten years earlier Fiedler had come to Birmingham from Leipzig to hold the chair of German in the old Mason's College, which had been assimilated into the new university at the turn of the century. (Some thirty-six years later this same Hermann Fiedler, a tutor to the Prince of Wales and editor of the *Oxford Book of German Poetry*, which would long remain in print, would be the mediator in a complicated episode of patronage in the career of Vaughan Williams.)

Doubtless Elgar felt honoured by the invitation initiated for him by those eminent figures in the cultural life of Birmingham, but when the offer was first broached he worried that the lectures he would be required to give would divert too much time from his composing. Perhaps too, as someone who had completed his formal education by the age of fifteen, he may have had doubts about his ability to assume a senior academic role. But the innate self-belief that sustained Elgar in his worst episodes of self-doubt prevailed on this occasion too and he accepted the professorship. In a preliminary note to one of the lectures his confidence expressed itself in an aggressive dismissal of 'the educated', those from whom 'no amount of education, no amount of the polish of university can eradicate the stain from the low type of mind we call commonplace'.

The lectures that Elgar delivered as Peyton Professor of Music in the University of Birmingham were edited by the energetic Midlands musicologist, football enthusiast and friend of Vaughan Williams, Percy M. Young. The lectures in one clear respect are a salute to Birmingham, an expression of gratitude for opportunities in time past and suggestions for improvements to the musical culture of the city, as part of what was proposed in the title of the first lecture, 'A Future for English Music'. Specifically, he wanted to help 'to make Birmingham, musically, a place it was worth the while of a student to live in'. Throughout the lectures there is an insistence on the local.

In that same first lecture, given many years before the concoction of the County of West Midlands, Elgar declares himself to be very conscious of 'standing on Warwickshire land'. Right at the beginning, in his second paragraph, he declares that:

> I hold it a happy chance, or, as we are serious today, I will say a happy Providence which places the new movement in English music in that district of England which was parent to all that is bright, beautiful and good in the works of him who we know and love under the name of Shakespeare.[18]

As a professor in the new university he is quick to acknowledge and admire the achievement of the other institution in the city that had for years advanced higher musical education: 'at present nothing could be better than the teaching of the Music School of the Midland Institute under the direction of Mr Granville Bantock and the splendid staff of professors.' He prophesied that 'the University and the Music School of the Institute will work in perfect harmony and goodwill.'[19]

Elgar was a great admirer of Granville Bantock, a composer some eleven years younger than himself who had progressed from conducting an itinerant comic opera company to becoming director of concerts at the New Brighton Tower. He then became principal of the school of music at the Birmingham and Midland Institute, which had been founded in 1854. Elgar dedicated the second of the *Pomp and Circumstance* marches to him. It was Bantock who appointed the distinguished music critic and journalist Ernest Newman to be a lecturer at the Institute. Newman also wrote for a time for the *Birmingham Daily Post* and his correspondence with Elgar offers a revealing commentary on the composer's creative career. With these three figures established in Birmingham, the musical life of the city had a brilliant nucleus.

With the painful disappointment of the *Gerontius* premiere now years behind him, Professor Elgar was now ready to acknowledge his indebtedness to William Stockley, who had given decades to developing and improving the quality of choral music in Birmingham, announcing to his well-to-do audience, 'I look back in pride and gratitude to my connection with the Festival Choral Society and that I was able to learn something of choral effect in the old days under our revered chief, Mr Stockley.'[20]

Elgar proposed to his audience that musical culture was made up of three constituents: composers, executants and critics (as three of his principal lectures were titled). He singled out three contemporary composers for commendation. One was Josef Holbrooke, today a largely forgotten figure who had begun his career playing in music halls and as a result of his compositions had gone on to be another of Granville Bantock's appointments in the music department of the Birmingham and Midland Institute. Elgar also mentioned Walford Davies, whose best-known work would be the very popular *Royal Air Force March Past* (1918). The year before Elgar delivered his lectures Walford Davies, who was then organist and choirmaster at the Temple Church in the City of London, had achieved a considerable success with his cantata *Everyman*, based on the fifteenth-century morality play. It was a popular subject at the time; six years later Hugo von Hofmannsthal, who had just written the first two of his six libretti for Richard Strauss, also had a success with his treatment of the story. Walford Davies would have other popular successes and go on to become a well-known broadcaster. On Elgar's death, Walford Davies succeeded him as Master of the King's Music.

The third composer to receive Elgar's commendation was another figure from the world of Birmingham music, Granville Bantock. At the time Elgar was giving his lectures, Bantock was working on his very ambitious choral epic *Omar Khayyám*, a setting of Edward FitzGerald's translation of the Persian poet's *Rubáiyát*, one of the best-known and best-loved poetry collections of late Victorian and Edwardian times. Elgar saw these three composers, all a few years younger than himself, as the transmitters of a revitalized tradition, a new resonance in English music. He told his audience that 'these men, Walford Davies, Holbrooke and Bantock, are making their way sturdily and opening the doors for the more juvenile composers upon whom we expect the burden to fall next.'[21]

In his lecture on 'English Executants', that is to say instrumentalists and performers, Elgar again stressed the local. William Stockley was once more acknowledged, this time for his achievements in developing the city's Festival Orchestra. Commenting on what he generally regarded as a high level of performance in the country, Elgar commented that 'In Birmingham, Mr Stockley paved the way for the present orchestra's work and it would be easy to name many who made noble efforts to improve the stagnant state of music.'[22] Elgar also admired the skill of English organists, who were so crucial in ecclesiastical and choral music. Charles Perkins, the organist of the City of Birmingham and a teacher at the Birmingham and Midland Institute, was at the top of the profession. Elgar's assessment of him was confident and unqualified: 'Our leading church organists are among the best and we have concert performers able to hold their own anywhere – and we need not go out of Birmingham for a shining example.'[23]

The *Birmingham Daily Post* also played a part in the local music culture that Elgar saw his professorship as designed to enhance. In his lecture entitled 'Critics' he stressed the important role of audiences in musical life: 'intelligent audiences [are] among the factors necessary to the working and well-being of a concrete art.' Especially important are those in audiences who write in the press about performances. But if Elgar was confident about the high calibre of executants in England, he was far less sure about the quality of published discussion of music. 'Critics of music have, in this country, a difficult task,' he told his listeners, 'inasmuch as this work has to be hurriedly displayed, or in the opinion of newspaper editors, its value ceases.'[24] Fast, deadline-meeting reviewing was no substitute for considered and serious published discussion. He lamented that

> we have no musical review, a periodical devoting itself to the considera-
> tion of music and matters bearing upon music apart from concert giving
> and concert going … English people do not read much about music except
> in snippets … Attempts to correct the situation have failed; we have seen
> during the last thirty years, the inauguration and disappearance of several
> periodicals devoting themselves to the art in the way I have mentioned.

All that Elgar feels able to do by way of conclusion is to single out journalists who, he believes, have in the difficult circumstances he describes, written criticism that has been helpful and creative for the development of the art form. Before so doing he considers the notorious difficulty attaching to the writing of responses to music in words. But there are some who make a creditable attempt to do so. The names of the music journalists he goes on to commend are mostly forgotten, except perhaps by the most special-ized of music historians, but there is one who made a significant literary contribution to Elgar's musical development – and indeed to that of Vaughan Williams and Benjamin Britten. This was Ernest Newman, who is rightly described in *The New Grove Dictionary of Music and Musicians* as 'the most celebrated British music critic in the first half of the twentieth century'.

For a number of years Ernest Newman wrote for the *Birmingham Daily Post*. He was very much part of the intensifying musical life in the city at this time. In 1903 Granville Bantock invited him to teach music theory at the Birmingham and Midland Institute. Two years later he left Birmingham to write music criticism for the *Manchester Guardian*, where he quickly attracted attention for his unhesitating and sometimes outspoken criticism of some of the music he heard there. Newman had much in common with the great literary critic F.R. Leavis, not least in their pre-eminence in their fields. Both could be trenchant, dismissive and provoking in their judgements; but both were unquestionably serious, responsible and dedicated in their long endeavours to illuminate and promote what was valuable and life-enhancing in the arts they wrote about. Along with one of the earliest studies of Elgar, published in 1906, Newman's numerous books on music include studies of Hugo Wolf and Richard Strauss, and a four-volume *Life of Richard Wagner*.

For all his admiration for Elgar's music, Newman would at times point to its failings. Elgar, in his lecture entitled 'Critics', maintained that this in no way hindered the necessary interaction between artist and critic: 'it is true we don't agree on several points, but I have never found differences of opinion makes daily interaction with real strong men less possible.'[25] Referring to what was to be Newman's brief departure to Manchester, Elgar expressed his unqualified esteem for his writings: 'I speak with admiration of a critic gone from among us, Mr Ernest Newman – a champion of the new school and an author of repute; it is a great regret to me that he has left Birmingham to take up an important post "somewhere further north".'

The last accentuated phrase will surely have brought smiles, if not laughter, from the audience, for it is an echo of a much-quoted remark from a letter from Elgar printed in the *Musical Times* in July 1903. In this he made fun of the 'sleepy London press' and went on to say, 'Some day the press will awake to the fact, already known abroad and to some few of us in London, that the living centre of music is not London, but somewhat further (*sic*) North.'[26]

In identifying, championing, and seeking to foster this 'living centre', by which he surely means Birmingham, Elgar is silent and modest about his own contribution to it. Of a comparison that was sometimes made between him and Beethoven, he told his listeners 'Let me say definitely that when I see one of my own works by the side of, say, the Fifth Symphony, I feel like a tinker may do when surveying the Forth Bridge, or as a mason when he sees ... the Campanile of the new Birmingham University.'[27] This second simile is an acknowledgement of the high clock tower, very much a public marvel, which at that very time was being constructed at Edgbaston on the south-western side of Birmingham. It was built as a tribute to Joseph Chamberlain, a great benefactor to the university and a former mayor of the city who had gone on to be one of the most prominent and controversial figures in national politics at the end of the nineteenth century and beyond. The campanile, the highest free-standing clock tower in the world and known as 'Old Joe', was designed by Sir Aston Webb, who was to the architecture of the Edwardian period what Elgar was to its music. In 1909 Webb's Victoria and Albert Museum was opened and in the same year he would complete Admiralty Arch beside Trafalgar Square. A few years later Webb would reface the frontage of Buckingham Palace to create the image known worldwide.

The campanile of Birmingham University, modelled to some extent on that of the Palazzo Pubblico in Siena, was part of the intellectual expansionism and confidence of Birmingham and indeed of the whole nation at this time. Elgar concluded his planned series of lectures with one entitled 'A Retrospect', assuring his listeners that music could and should be part of this. One of his final paragraphs was just one simple, emphatic sentence: 'We know the position England held musically in Purcell's time and earlier: that position was soon lost, it can be regained.'[28]

Elgar ascribed the debilitation of English music in the nineteenth century in part to a lack of investment and interest in provincial places. He ended his series of lectures with a ringing hope that this could now be remedied:

> The establishment in the eighteenth century of numerous orchestras in all the little Capitals (*sic*) of Germany had the greatest effect in fostering, and in many cases creating, a love for orchestral music. We had at that period no such help to a musical life. But we may hope that if all true artists, composers, executants and critics work together, setting aside small differences of opinion, we may once again be a musical land and produce a 'school' (not an egotism of several) of serious English music which shall have a hold on the affections of the people and SHALL (sic) be held in respect abroad.

Elgar completed his first series of lectures but found the preparation hard going. By the autumn of 1907 he felt that he could not go on to give a further series. Ernest Newman was one of those, including Walford Davies, who took his place for one of the seven formal occasions that had been planned for the University's grandest venue, the Large Lecture Theatre in the sooty Gothic building on Edmund Street. Newman spoke of 'New Forms in Music', one of which was a new type of art being presently devised by Elgar. 'His idea,' Newman reported, 'was for a new combination of orchestra, acting and pictures', though conceding that 'the idea was not exactly new. Liszt had thought of using it in his *Dante Symphony*, the pictures being thrown upon a screen.' Perhaps it was the inventive, entrepreneurial ethos of turn-of-the-century Birmingham that motivated Elgar to contemplate such new technological possibilities for the music arts – a serious amateur chemist, he also quickly interested himself in the developing recording industry – but nothing came of the new art form that he had discussed with Newman. The responsibilities of the professorship now clearly weighed him down. On 31 July 1906 he noted in his diary that he was 'depressed at Birmingham prospects'. A few weeks later he wrote a letter of resignation from the professorship and felt 'a weight lifted'.

In this way Elgar's association with Birmingham for well over a quarter of a century petered out, and with it an important stage in his career as a composer. Henceforth his finest energies would not be directed into choral writing but rather into compositions for orchestra.

There had, however, been one last grand choral (and social) occasion in the city some eighteen months before he gave up the Peyton professorship: the premiere in Birmingham Town Hall of *The Kingdom*, the sequel to *The Apostles*. The excitement generated by this first performance of the new oratorio matched that which had greeted its predecessor. The *Birmingham Daily Post* reported what was a high point in the parabola of Elgar's celebrity,

> The Town Hall never presented a more crowded aspect at a Festival than it did this morning. There was not a corner in the great hall that was not occupied, right from the organ loft to the extreme end of the great gallery. It testified to the popularity of the great English composer, the man of the hour, who has instituted a new art form in oratorio.

The new work continued the epic story of the emergence of Christianity. It begins with a Prelude, *allegro maestoso*, that recalls the music that had accompanied Christ's last words to the Apostles, 'Go ye therefore and teach all nations.' Then the music goes on to evoke and illustrate five episodes from the Acts of the Apostles. The first takes place 'In the Upper Room', where the disciples assemble to sing a simple hymn and to choose the new apostle, Matthias, to take the place of Judas Iscariot. 'At the Beautiful Gate' is dominated by the voices of the two Marys, as with a Homeric simplicity they recall some of the extraordinary acts of Jesus. The third part is a musically intense evocation of 'Pentecost'. The choral writing gathers pace as the contralto soloist dramatically announces, 'And suddenly there came from heaven a sound of the rushing of a mighty wind', leading to a climax with a characteristically epic moment in which the Divine intervenes in human life as the Mystic Chorus of sopranos and contraltos declare, 'The Lord put forth His hand and touched their mouth.'

There follows a section entitled 'The Sign of Healing' in which Saints Peter and John are imprisoned after demonstrating their God-given powers by healing the lame man. In the final episode we are again in 'The Upper Room' after the freeing of Peter and John, when the disciples celebrate the divinity that has pervaded the work by breaking bread together and singing the Lord's Prayer.

Critics of the early performances found *The Kingdom* episodic, discontinuous and lacking in a properly and organically evolved finale. The reviewer in the *Daily News*, for instance, objected that 'the oratorio could not end at what seems a natural conclusion. But having that intention, Sir Edward Elgar ought surely to have planned his music on different lines.'[29] Ernest Newman, reviewing *The Kingdom* for the *Birmingham Daily Post*, was also disappointed by the music: 'Some of the choral portions are so obvious in sentiment that one could hardly believe they came from the delicately spiritual brain that conceived "Gerontius".' In an article for the same newspaper a few months later, however, Newman wrote a far more radical and devastating criticism of Elgar's grand project, one that foretold correctly that Elgar's musical vision was not epic, but rather lyric:

He has seen fit to fasten on his own back the burden of an unwieldy, impossible scheme for three oratorios on the subject of the founding of the Church, and until that scheme is done with, and Elgar seeks inspiration in a subject of another type, the most sanguine of us cannot expect much from him in the way of fresh or really vital music.

The wisest thing for him to do now is to abandon the idea of a third oratorio on the subject and turn his mind to other themes. These may bring him new inspiration and a new idiom; at present he is simply riding post-haste along the road that leads to nowhere.[30]

We do not know whether Elgar read or considered the views and advice of this friend and distinguished music critic in 1907, but it is clear that over time he finally came to share them: the third part of the epic trilogy, *The Last Judgement*, was never completed. Some twenty years after the first performance of *The Kingdom* Elgar's daughter Carice noted, 'Father full of writing Apostles III'.[31] But this is one of the rare and very intermittent indications of Elgar's serious engagement with the completion of his grand epic project. Very soon after completing *The Kingdom* he seems to have lost confidence in his ability to complete his most ambitious choral project.

Over the years friends and supporters recurrently attempted to help him return to it. Six years after the premiere of *The Kingdom*, Ivor Atkins, at that time the organist of Worcester Cathedral, offered him a commission to complete the trilogy for the Three Choirs Festival in Worcester in 1914, but the proposal came to nothing. Six years later another old friend, the violinist Billy Reed, attempted to encourage Elgar to resume work on his sequence of oratorios.

I tried once or twice to lead him on by asking him about the third part of the Trilogy ... He had a cupboard full of sketch-work for it; and once or twice I succeeded in getting him to play me some of it, in the hope that I should set him on fire once more and get him to complete the trilogy. But I could not stay with him all the time; and the moment I went away, it all went back into the cupboard and nothing was done.[32]

One of Elgar's wealthy supporters later in his career was the successful Yorkshire industrialist Henry Embleton. He took a more robust approach to inducing Elgar to complete what the composer called his 'GIGANTIC WORX'. In 1920 Embleton sent Elgar a cheque for £500, which he described as a loan against the completion of *The Last Judgement*. Elgar cashed the cheque. Some years later, in the first week of February 1930, Henry Embleton died and his executors were shocked to find that, for all his wealth, he had nearly bankrupted himself in his passionate support of choral music. They found it difficult to cover the estate's obligations and wrote to Elgar requesting the return of the £500 loan. This was just after Black Tuesday in New York, when the Stock Market on Wall Street crashed so momentously. Elgar found it difficult to raise the money but eventually succeeded. His inability to sustain his epic vision, however, brought a very material blow as well as the pain of an artistic failure.

Just a few months after repaying his debt to the Embleton estate Elgar encountered Vaughan Williams at the Three Choirs Festival at Hereford. Elgar's disappointment and pain at not completing *The Last Judgement* must have been intensified most poignantly by hearing Vaughan Williams's oratorio *Sancta Civitas* played at the festival together with his own *The Kingdom*, for Vaughan Williams's oratorio in effect presents the final chapter of the account of Christian history that Elgar himself had once promised to set. In a BBC broadcast of 1957 the younger composer recalled Elgar's great dignity and generosity on that day in Hereford more than a quarter of a century earlier:

> He came to hear a performance of my *Sancta Civitas* and gave it generous praise. He told me that he had once thought of setting these words himself. 'But I shall never do it now', he said. To this I could only answer that this made me sorry that I had ever attempted to set the words myself.[33]

Michael Kennedy, in his biography of Vaughan Williams, points out that with 'becoming modesty' Vaughan Williams did not quote Elgar's remarks in full. They included the words, 'I once thought of setting these words, but I shall never do that now, and I am glad I didn't because you have done it for me.'[34]

The occasion demonstrates touchingly that continuity of epic concerns that informs the careers of the first two great composers of the English musical renaissance. Both continued to return to history as a subject, together with the superhuman powers that drive history and man's capacity for the heroic within it. Their concern with history as a subject would be taken up, albeit in very different musical forms, by Benjamin Britten.

The forms that Elgar and Vaughan Williams employed in their endeavours to give sound to epic processes were derived from the traditions of choral music. However it is not primarily for their choral works that these two composers are remembered and performed. They are esteemed more for their orchestral works. Choral music that has a close bonding with words is essentially programme music and Elgar could not complete his twentieth-century understanding of the Christian epic in these terms. Certainly he aspired to look out beyond himself and give an account of Christian history. But his finest, deepest musical insights were into his own private experience and best expressed through the purer, supra-verbal music of the symphony.

Vaughan Williams's choral ambitions were never as vast as those pursued by Elgar in his proposed trilogy, though he did take up the great theme of Christian eschatology in *Sancta Civitas*. Yet the profoundest moments in his music occur in his symphonies. And as we consider the complete sequence of his nine symphonies we can say that, although Vaughan Williams cannot at the outset have planned a sequence, the nine works taken together do give us a personal account, one man's inner history of English experience in the momentous first half of the twentieth century. Elgar composed only two complete symphonies but within a shorter historical range the same can also be said of him. The symphony was his form of refuge after his large notion of a tripartite oratorio had proved unworkable. Paradoxically, as Elgar turned to this less programmatic orchestral music and to the articulation of his own most private experience, he produced artefacts that together tell of a historic turning point. His two symphonies are in one important respect a sensitive registering of the ultimate destruction of an important feature of pre-twentieth century consciousness in Britain, the High Tory ideal.

☙

The first great orchestral work of Elgar's career was the *Enigma Variations* of 1898. It belonged to, and can be seen as, the creative climax of the West Midlands or Birmingham phase of his development as a composer. As he completed the famous piece, his family had settled into a far grander home than they had recently been accustomed to, a larger, newer detached house on the upper side of the Wells Road beyond Great Malvern. Craeg Lea, as they called their new home, represented a social and psychological as well as a geographical distancing from the area in which he had struggled so long to establish himself. Birmingham was now an incidental part of his outlook. From the large first-floor window that lit his study he could, he told readers of the *Strand Magazine*, 'see across Worcestershire to Edgehill, the Cathedral of Worcester, the abbeys of Pershore and Tewkesbury and even the smoke from around Birmingham'.[35] The second city was now a distant place.

As Elgar removed himself from his origins, the more his music turned inward into a concern with his own inner life. Ostensibly the *Enigma Variations*, like most of the choral narratives of earlier years, looks outward. It is about a group of acquaintances, friends 'pictured within', a social milieu in fact. Of the fourteen characters from the early Malvern years that make up this portrait gallery, however, the composer himself, alluded to as E.D.U., the name by which Elgar was known to his wife, receives by far the largest amount of attention. In a piece that lasts just over half an hour, he receives well over five minutes, more than any of the other characters. Elgar himself is the grand conclusion to the party – and his wife it is who greets us at the very beginning. If there may be a slight hint of *égoïsme à deux* in this, the expression and assertion of the Elgarian ego in the final variation is all the more pre-eminent. The final variation is extended and it is joyous and proud.

In the early days of the Romantic movement John Keats identified what he termed 'the egotistical sublime' as the characterizing feature of the poetry of one of the movement's founders, William Wordsworth. The concern with and celebration of selfhood that Keats described continued through the late romantic into the modernist movement. The title of one of modernism's most important periodicals, *The Egoist*, continues the insistence on a way of perceiving that resists the conventional, the established and the subordination of the individual. This historic magazine was founded in 1911 by the determined feminist Dora Marsden, with the title *The Freewoman*. It then, with the financial assistance of the great literary patroness Harriet Shaw Weaver, became *The New Freewoman* and then, in January 1914, *The Egoist*. The new title was in part inspired by an influential book about psychology, Max Stirner's *The Ego and its Own* (1845). The highly progressive and original poet Ezra Pound was appointed to be the literary editor of the magazine and through his astute initiatives *The Egoist* published some of the founding texts of modernist literature: poetry by D.H. Lawrence and James Joyce's *Portrait of the Artist as a Young Man* were followed by a serialization of chapters from Joyce's highly controversial novel *Ulysses*. *The Egoist* also published important work by T.S. Eliot, William Carlos Williams and Ezra Pound himself.

These young modernist pioneers were no great admirers of Elgar. (In the short-lived periodical *Blast*, produced in 1914–15 during the Vorticist phase of modernism in literature, sculpture and painting, Elgar is one in a long list of those 'blasted'.) He, in turn, would surely have had no interest in the young artists published under the masthead of *The Egoist*. Nevertheless he did share with these figures of a later generation a profound concern with the self and its evolution. And though, among American poets, it was Longfellow and his narratives that he read and admired rather than Longfellow's far greater contemporary Walt Whitman, he shared with Whitman that intense preoccupation that directed 'Song of Myself'. Elgar's five greatest orchestral works were all produced after he uprooted himself from his native West Midlands and ceased musicalizing historical narratives. Henceforth, his greatest works, and they are orchestral rather than choral, were songs of himself rather than stories of a larger humanity. The five are: the *Enigma Variations*, the two symphonies and the violin and cello concertos. The founding poet of English romanticism, William Wordsworth, gave to his historic long poem *The Prelude* the subtitle *Growth of a Poet's Mind*. Elgar's five principal works for instruments are also, at their core, accounts of this composer's mind. The verbal and literary annotations that he attached to these five works clearly indicate and particularize the chapters of autobiography that are their chief subject.

The *Enigma Variations* was composed around the time that Richard Strauss was beginning to write *Ein Heldenleben*, another work of blatant self-commendation. There is nothing to suggest that either work affected the other but together they help to confirm that there was a spirit in the time that favoured the assertion of artistic selfhood. The concluding bars of the *Enigma Variations* are a fanfare of self-proclamation, but our sense, as listeners, is that this is in no way vulgar self-glorification. It is a joyous celebration of the composer, certainly, but it is also a celebration of the remarkable people who have made for that joyousness and it is also the celebration of the concluding and completion of a work of art.

The *Enigma Variations* is a marvel of compression. Within it there are succinctly evoked and sounded a great variety not just of recollected individual characteristics but of human feelings, attitudes, moods, deportments, postures and mannerisms. Benjamin Britten would surely not have had this work in mind when he selected and set passages from Arthur Rimbaud's *Les Illuminations*, but the basic autobiographical method and design is very similar. Each of the fourteen characters portrayed in the *Enigma Variations* is clearly individualized and multifaceted. The more we listen to the piece, the more we are aware of its detailing.

But at the same time the overall piece is clearly based on the kind of dualisms that are potentially symphonic. One group of characters, Ysobel (Isabel Fitton) of the sixth variation, W.N. or Winifred Norbury of the ninth and B.G.N. or Basil Nevinson of the twelfth, is portrayed by the music of the inner life. Their variations are delicate, gentle, dreamy, usually slow and at times tinged with melancholy. A striking, amusing contrast is first introduced by the loud thumping music lasting less than half a minute that gives us W.M.B. (William Meath Baker) whom his fellow variation Dorabella (Dora Penny) remembered as 'a small wiry man, very quick and energetic,' who 'had an incisive way of speaking – laying down the law sometimes'.[36] This theme of extraversion returns three variations later with the knockabout, thunder and lightning music of Elgar's architect friend Arthur Troyte Griffith, whom an onlooker described as 'that refreshing but highly argumentative Harrovian'.[37] And then after the stammering Dorabella's delicate little *pas seul* comes more sound, fury and bluster from the bulldog owner Dr George Robertson Sinclair.

Each of these human types, even the coarser, more extroverted ones, is endowed by the music with a number of characteristics and idiosyncrasies. The overall effect of this highly detailed diversity is to provoke similarly variegated responses in the listener. These range from amusement to sympathy, to indulgence, to respect, to reverence, to awe. The last two responses are the effects produced by the two variations that introduce and conclude the first third of the work. They pull together the seeming symphonic dualities that have recurred earlier in the piece. The first is *Nimrod*, the famous passage that is a salute to August Jaeger, Elgar's trusted friend and publisher at Novello in London. This variation begins in the mood and style of the gentler ones that have come earlier. It is a music that ponders and reflects and then, unlike anything before it in the piece, moves into a noble melody that mounts slowly into a grand climax. This is the first great emotional summit of the work. It makes way for the shy, slightly stammering but also very charming entry of the youthful Dorabella. With the Jaeger variation, however, we have the first great *nobilmente* in Elgar's orchestral compositions. It is an affecting, memorializing tribute to this loyal, understanding, supportive friend and to that tradition of Austro-German music to which he was, for Elgar, an important bridge.

The evocation and celebration of what is noble in life is also a pronounced feature of Elgar's self-portrait in the very final variation. But it is surely qualified by an accompanying admission of showiness that is another feature of the variation. The consequence is to make the Nimrod section stand out, in our remembering of the work, as the noblest image of humanity in its multitudinous variation as portrayed in the work.

If Jaeger's unqualified nobility is the finest feature of life that sounds out from among the *Enigma Variations*, this quality returns again as one of the prime dualities that constitute the subject and direct the organization of Elgar's First Symphony of 1908. The work is a highly subjective, lyrical piece. In a letter he remarked that 'I am really alone in this Music' and in another he wrote of it as 'a reflex or picture of elucidation' of his life. It was first performed approximately a decade after the *Enigma Variations*. These ten years were ones in which Elgar had employed his best musical energies in an epic purpose, the setting of the story of the intervention of the Christian God into human affairs and the aftermath of this intervention and Incarnation. But, as we have noted, after the qualified success of *The Apostles* and *The Kingdom* his desire to complete the sequence of epic oratorios faltered and eventually failed. He then gave rein to the promptings of his lyrical, autobiographical impulses, which had shown themselves in the *Enigma Variations* and now found fuller, deeper expression in the symphony.

Elgar had a brilliant success with his first completed venture into the form. After the work had its first London performance on 7 December 1908 in the Queen's Hall in Portland Place under the distinguished German conductor Hans Richter. Jaeger described the audience response in a letter to Dora Penny:

> I never in all my experience saw the like. The Hall was *packed* ... The atmosphere was electric ... After the first movement E.E. was called out; again, several times, after the third, and then came the great moment. After the superb Coda (Finale) the audience seemed to rise at E. when he appeared. I never heard such frantic applause after any novelty nor such shouting. Five times he had to appear before they were pacified. People stood up and even *on* their seats to get a view ...[38]

Richter shared the enthusiasm of the audience and his admiration for the new symphony was profound. He told the orchestra that they were playing 'the greatest symphony of modern times, and not only in this country'. When they came to rehearse the Adagio this associate of Johannes Brahms exclaimed, 'Ah! This is a *real* Adagio such as Beethoven would have written.' As Richter implicitly prophesied, the achievement represented by the First Symphony was by no means parochial. The work had a wildfire success worldwide, receiving performances in Australia, America, Germany and Russia. The resurgence of English music was underway.

The symphony was worked on and completed in the years following the historic, landslide defeat of the Tories at the general election of 1906. For some such as Vaughan Williams and his friends this event, which staggered British society, was, as we will see, an occasion for joyous excitement, an encouragement, a stimulus, a liberation. But for those like Elgar who held to the High Tory view of life this great turning point of a general election was cause for a profound sense of loss and an enduring sense of melancholy with regard to the future state of the nation. The principles of High Toryism – an adherence to chivalric ideals, a belief in a hierarchical ordering of society informed by the assumption of *noblesse oblige*, a belief in paternalistic community rather than the atomized society of evolving capitalism – are all very visible in the literature of this time. They underpin the delicately sustained ironic vision of Joseph Conrad, Elgar's exact contemporary, in his great novels *Nostromo* and *The Secret Agent*. The High Tory vision and lament were maintained by writers of a later generation such as T.S. Eliot and Evelyn Waugh. Ford Madox Ford, author of *The Good Soldier*, one of the most perfectly fashioned novels of the twentieth century, also wrote an extended account of the challenges and pains experienced by a High Tory sensibility in the new, democratizing and feminizing society of the twentieth century. This is his tetralogy *Parade's End*. The four novels, *Some Do Not ...*, *No More Parades*, *A Man Could Stand Up* and *Last Post*, tell the story of a brilliant, well-intentioned aristocrat, Christopher Tietjens, referred to as 'the last Tory'. He is the kind of high-born man and socially well-placed figure that Elgar started to socialize with after his long delayed artistic success, which took him away from Birmingham and its hinterland and the more modestly placed friends he had known in and around Malvern. (One of his new close friends was the Marquess of Northampton.)

The word nobility can have two meanings: it can refer either to a social group or to a moral quality. As he composed his first symphony, Elgar was starting to hobnob with the first, while the second meaning was an important desideratum within High Tory ideals, which he showed, in his symphony, to be very much under threat. History sees changes in moral emphases and priorities: the young Benjamin Britten would be irritably impatient with Elgar's dwelling on, and assertion of *nobilmente*. 'Andante. Nobilmente e semplice – Allegro' is Elgar's title for the first movement of his first symphony. *Nobilmente* is the great positive in the work, the ideal that will be alluded to in different tones and orchestral textures throughout the piece and one which, after many and various vicissitudes, will be triumphantly proclaimed at the rousing conclusion.

The music of the opening, the first statement of *nobilmente*, is slow, stately, lofty and endowed with a beautiful poise. The nobility theme is repeated and amplified inspiringly. But overall within this first movement, it fades. A final exhaustion in fact marks the ending of all three movements. One theme of the work is the struggle to assert value musically in the face of an enveloping world weariness. The symphony, we recall, was composed close to the *fin de siècle* and to the mood of exhaustion that pervaded the arts at that time.

But the very first challenge that confronts the opening *nobilmente* is not this; it is a music in D minor that expresses perturbation, hurry and instability. The fine poise is utterly lost. There is a pause for some moments of wistful regret but then the turbulence returns even more violently. *Nobilmente* flickers in again, the first of three very different reappearances in this first movement. But now it does not have its opening authority. There are quivering uncertainties, then a recovering of a certain elan that soon degenerates into discordances. How is the great ideal to be stuck to and lived out? *Nobilmente*, gently but briefly, insinuates itself again. But a steadfast adherence to the high and beautiful ideal is not possible. Disorder returns, giving way to sadness. *Nobilmente* re-enters, with more strength this time, but finally falls away into regret and weariness. For the moment, at the break signalling the end of the movement, the dialogue, or perhaps more accurately, the conflict between the high ideal and troubling, even distressing, contingencies is ended by exhaustion.

The second movement, Allegro molto, the shortest of the four, sounds out everyday experience. It is, to begin with, the music of the various things that make up daily life. There is a scurrying about and then a resolute purposeful march that accelerates into the brazen. But then comes the sound of a clock winding down. This sounding of mortality dissipates, making irrelevant the energetic activities of daily life. The music of different kinds of distraction ends in weariness. The concluding bars of this Allegro molto are ones of exhaustion, the inevitable finale of the things of this world.

The third movement, the Adagio acclaimed by Hans Richter, is indeed one of Elgar's most affecting symphonic movements. It begins with a succession of sighs, slow and protracted, which only very slowly rise to a mood of brightness. Then halfway through comes a beautiful elegiac melody. It is a moving expression of the depths of regret from which the effort to recover *nobilemente* has to begin. There is just one, gentle, somewhat remote hint of the ideal being remembered before the sadness returns and the music fades wistfully away. Even regret, however deep, can wear itself out. Like the two preceding movements the Adagio finally dwindles into silence.

The fourth and final movement, Lento – Allegro, takes up the basic dualism in the work, *nobilmente* and its subverters, with some uncertainty. The opening bars are murky. *Nobilmente* is remembered for a moment but it now sounds tentative. Ominousness takes over. *Nobilmente* is heard again but in a disfigured form. There is a sense of loss, but determination then sets in. The pace suddenly quickens; purpose returns and sweeps on. *Nobilmente* joins in, now matching the resolution, and the music continues to gather momentum to the point of triumph again. But the music of high idealism is also assailed by hostile chatter. (The conflict is very similar to that heard at the ending of the overture to Wagner's *Tannhäuser*.) But the malign shrillnesses are conclusively dominated by the *nobilmente* theme and, as the last chords approach, there comes the exhilarating feeling of the composer's ultimate, excited triumph.

~

Some four months after the first performance of his First Symphony Elgar was at work on what was to prove his third great orchestral work, his Violin Concerto in B minor. If the symphony investigated two conflicting facts of experience, two ways of viewing life, the Violin Concerto refocuses the duality in a much more personalized and particularized fashion. The most blatantly autobiographical of all his great orchestral works, it is essentially a protracted love song. It is about the reconciliation of love's intensities with the mundanity that calls them into question. It is also a dialogue between two lovers – or far more probably between two would-be lovers. Or two lovers who, given their social situations (each was married) and under the dictates of chivalry, find their consummation, like that of so many nineteenth-century heroes and heroines of fiction and opera, in the profound poignancy of renunciation.

There can be little doubt that Elgar's wife Alice was the prime and sustaining relationship of his life. But it is also clear from his letters and the biographies that, with his wife's tolerant indulgence, he contracted on an emotional level intense relationships with other women. There are a number of accounts of affairs in which Elgar was involved and even rumours of an illegitimate daughter. However this may be, it is beyond question that no relationship with a woman outside his marriage affected Elgar more than that which developed between him and Alice Stuart-Wortley, which reached its highest intensity during the year 1910 as he composed the Violin Concerto.

She was the wife of Charles Stuart-Wortley, the Conservative MP for Sheffield Hallam. It seems likely that she first met Elgar in 1902 when he conducted *Gerontius* at the Sheffield Festival. Like Elgar, Alice was younger than her spouse, she by some eleven years. Her aristocratic husband, educated at Rugby School and then Balliol College, Oxford, had gone on to become a successful barrister and pursued a steady, if not brilliant career in the parliamentary Conservative Party. The signs are that he was emotionally distanced from his younger wife.

In becoming a close friend of Alice Stuart-Wortley Elgar came into association with a leading and conspicuous, if not notorious, family in the arts in Britain in the late nineteenth century. Alice's mother was Effie Gray, whose marriage to the eminent writer and critic John Ruskin had been annulled on the grounds of 'incurable impotency' in 1854. She subsequently married John Everett Millais, one of the painters who founded the Pre-Raphaelite Brotherhood. She had eight children by him, the fifth being Alice, who was born some five years after Elgar. Like her husband, Alice was passionately interested in music and she became a keen admirer of Elgar's work and the friendship between the Stuart-Wortleys and the Elgars became closer. When in 1904 there was a celebratory, three-day festival of Elgar's music at Covent Garden, an occasion that confirmed his national celebrity beyond question, the Stuart-Wortleys organized a dinner in his honour at their grand house designed by Norman Shaw in Cheyne Walk, Chelsea. As the intimacy between the two couples grew, Alice and Edward spent time alone together in the spring of 1909. The relationship between the two of them was beginning to bypass the social conventions of the day. He also began to address her in letters by her first name instead of by her title as a married woman. Less than a year later, as he worked on the Violin Concerto, he felt sufficiently established in her life to be able to rename her in the light of his personal perception of her. She became his Windflower. What her husband thought of this new endearment is not known.

Years later Elgar explained what the windflower, sometimes known as the *Anemone nemorosa*, meant to him:

> Windflowers, when the east wind rasps over the ground in March and April, merely turn their backs and bow before the squall. They are buffeted and blown, as one may think almost to destruction; but their anchors hold, and the slender-looking stems bend but do not break. And when the rain clouds drive up the petals shut tight into a tiny tent, as country folk tell one, to shelter the little person inside.[39]

Resilience and a deeply concealed and protected sensibility would appear to be the characteristics that Elgar chose to identify in this new naming of Alice.

Her sensibility was a profoundly romantic one. A favourite place and one that she often visited was Tintagel on the north coast of Cornwall, one of the sites of the Arthurian legends and the Lyonesse of *Tristan und Isolde*, and of Thomas Hardy. Here Elgar visited the Stuart-Wortleys with some friends on 4 April 1910 and something happened between him and Alice that he would never forget. Twelve months later he wrote to her from Cincinnati, Ohio, which he regarded, like most of America, as 'a nightmare', and recalled the previous year and their day's outing from Tintagel to nearby Boscastle. Imagining her in Tintagel he wrote, 'I am selfish enough to be thankful that you can think of me there and you will not forget Frank's car taking us to Boscastle and you will not forget the road home – how lovely it was – a year ago! ... My love to you.'[40]

There is no evidence to explain what happened between the two of them on that spring day in the land of King Arthur. An admission, a declaration of love from one or both of them? Whatever it was, we know that for years afterwards he would have windflowers sent to her to commemorate the occasion. Given its long-lasting impact we may conclude that it was a profound emotional, perhaps spiritual experience that they shared that day. Its connection with the Violin Concerto is abundantly documented. Two days after the memorable experience he sent a postcard of Land's End on which he had written two of the climactic chords from the concerto. A fortnight later as he proceeded with the work he told her, 'I have been working hard at the windflower themes – but all stands still until you come and approve.' In a letter to her the following day he reported that, 'The tunes stick and are not windflowerish – at present.' When it turned out that he had a spare ticket for the first performance, he liked to imagine her taking over the conducting while he sat in the audience and, thanks to the happy accident of the spare ticket, heard her conducting the work in which she would be forever present. He wrote, 'I wish I could use it and you might conduct – but you *will* be conducting the concerto wherever you are.'

The concerto is dedicated to its first soloist, Fritz Kreisler, but the score also has an inscription in Spanish: 'A qui esta encerrada el alma de....', which may be translated as 'Herein is enshrined the soul of....' It is a quotation from *Gil Blas de Santillane* (1715–35), a famous French picaresque novel by Alain-René Lesage, who based his book on Spanish sources. The quotation appears on a sheet of Alice Stuart-Wortley's notepaper and there is surely little doubt that the five dots at the end of the inscription stand discreetly for her initials A.S.C.S.-W. The concerto is an echoing shrine for something that was lost, or more likely, never could be.

49

The concerto is in many of its passages an elegiac love song. At times it can also sound like a narrative, and at others like a duet in which the spirit of the windflower is expressed by the violin and Elgar's various responses, as an entranced lover, by the orchestra. The opening bars of the first movement, the Allegro, are Elgar at his most outgoing, purposeful and brisk. But the second theme shows another and contrasting side to the orchestral character, marked by tenderness and long, lingering regret.

And then the violin responds echoing the tenderness with gentle under-standing. But her feelings then become more robust. In fact they build into a music of passion, a rhapsodic serenade. Buoyed by this there follows a duet in which gently, and lyrically, soloist and orchestra console and reassure each other. But then the violin takes charge. Alice Stuart-Wortley may have been a windflower but she was definitely not, the evidence indicates, a shrinking violet. The violin is now charged with a confidence and an intensity into which finally the orchestra is swept up. There is in this togetherness an excitement and a joy that approach ecstasy. As they crest and eventually fall away there is a quick, piercing remembrance of what is sad in the relationship of soloist and orchestra. But then with marked determination they come together in a triumphal happiness. The female voice of the violin gives the lead, speeding away. The orchestra, which at the beginning of the movement had a happy, breezy, macho self-confidence, now has to hurry to keep up.

The beginning of the second movement, the Andante, finds the orchestra subdued and thoughtful. The violin enters gently sympathizing. But finally the violin too concedes the presence of sadness and indeed descends deeper and deeper into it. Now it is the turn of the orchestra to attempt a rescue, to sympathize and to encourage, but the violin persists in its soulful probing. It engages in a lengthy soliloquy with condoling murmurs from the orchestra in the background. One long drawn-out note ends the Andante in a state of abstracted thoughtfulness.

Between the second and final movements there is a dramatic shift in mood and perspective as there had been between the second and first. At the beginning of the third and last movement the oppressed violin has recovered its spirits. It is excited again and celebratory. The orchestra joins in but not strongly enough for the violin, which is now insistent and persevering. Its joyousness is of a kind to infect the audience, but not for long because the orchestra turns again to sobering reflection. The violin, however, urges it out of this state and at last the two come together, abandoning themselves to the happiness that they have established in earlier movements as an indisputable aspect of their relationship.

Elgar himself said of the Violin Concerto that it was 'awfully emotional! Too emotional but I love it.' The piece is indeed very much about the dynamics of the emotions, about the ebb and flow of emotion between two people and about how the patterns of thought and feeling in one affect those in the other. The concerto is about that double stream of consciousness affecting two people who in difficult, even painful circumstances are in love with each other. Heard overall, however, the concerto presents and salutes the power of the figure whose soul 'Here is enshrined,' the windflower, as the prime and more joyously redemptive mover in the work. The very notion of the shrine refers to a locus of spirituality. It is a place of sacrifice and renunciation. These are both features of the chivalric ideal, which was an important part of the mental landscape of Elgar and those who shared his high Tory ideals.

Elgar's Second Symphony in E flat, like the Violin Concerto, was also very much a consequence of his relationship with Alice Stuart-Wortley. In letters to her over the many years of their friendship he would refer to it as 'your symphony'. In April 1909 Elgar visited Venice, a place that for him was a powerfully creative influence, as it would later be for Benjamin Britten. Here his ideas for his Second Symphony appear to have begun to consolidate. He wrote the word 'Venice' on the score, but beside it he also wrote the name of another place, Tintagel: that important occasion in his relationship with Alice Stuart-Wortley continued to inform this work as it had the Violin Concerto. In January 1911 he reported to her how he had made reference in the Second Symphony to their experience in Tintagel some nine months before: 'I have recorded last year in the first movement to which I put the last note in the score a moment ago and I must tell you this: I have worked at fever heat and the thing is tremendous in energy.'[41]

The Tintagel moment was surely one of those rare moments in Elgar's life in which he was visited by that 'Spirit of Delight' apostrophized by the Romantic poet Shelley in a poem entitled 'Song'. Elgar chose the first two lines of it as an epigraph for the Second Symphony. The first stanza reads:

Rarely, rarely, comest thou,
Spirit of Delight!
Wherefore hast thou left me now
Many a day and night?

Many a weary night and day
'Tis since thou art fled away.

In a letter to Ernest Newman, his old friend from Birmingham days, he wrote in May 1911 that, 'My attitude to the poem, or rather to the "Spirit of Delight", was an attempt to give the reticent Spirit a hint (with sad enough retrospection) as to what we should like to have.'

And did not have. And could not have. This was surely, in part, a full lover's relationship with Alice Stuart-Wortley. But the symphony has, of course, a much wider range of reference and implication. Like T.S. Eliot's *Four Quartets*, it is about the might have been and, more complicatedly, its effect on what actually has been. It ponders glimpses of joys that are curtailed by actuality and made the more precious by the relentlessness of time and mortality.

The symphony begins with the same brisk, surging confidence and happiness that marked the opening of the other work inspired by Alice Stuart-Wortley, the Violin Concerto. The exuberance is closely connected to what follows, a delicate, lyrical theme lucidly flowing. Here is the first intimation of the Spirit of Delight. This and its buoyant companion theme, 'tremendous in energy', must relate to the Tintagel experience that Elgar recalled to Alice Stuart-Wortley. But then comes the first setback, the sounds of what Elgar called 'a sort of malign influence wandering through the summer night in the garden'. On another occasion he put it differently. The passage, he wrote to a friend, 'might be a love scene in a garden at night when the ghost of some memory comes *through it*; – it makes me shiver.'[42] What then follows is a complex sequence of changes in consciousness that makes this symphony so much more intricate and difficult to follow than Elgar's First. The Second is very much a work of the twentieth century in that, like the symphonies of Mahler, Shostakovich and the later Vaughan Williams, it is in an important respect the sounding out of an eventful psychological journey.

After that first overshadowing of the Spirit of Delight there comes a reassertion of confidence, indeed a building up to a sense of triumph, but this cannot be sustained. The music becomes uncertain and diffident. There is uneasiness and eeriness. The instability of this musical and psychological situation is intensified by the first of the two clock chimes that are heard in this first movement.

There is more dawdling uncertainty before there comes a first and then a second resolution to recover the music of delight. The clock chimes give a second warning, but then after some moments of quiet pondering there comes at long last the triumphant recovery of what had been lost and then searched for throughout the movement.

However, such reclamations occur only within a larger and painful context. As Shelley wrote, reproachfully apostrophizing the Spirit of Delight with a tortuous highly particularized simile:

> As a lizard with the shade
> Of a trembling tent,
> Though with sorrow art dismayed;
> Even the sighs of grief
> Reproach thee, that thou are not near,
> And reproach thou wilt not hear.

Grieving and a sense of loss are the themes of the second movement, the Larghetto. It begins with the slow, heavy tread of a funeral march. Waves of tremulous feeling then alternate with the inexorable beat of the slow music. A quiet, very deliberate pondering is followed by nervous stabbing pulsations. Elgar described the passage, again to Ernest Newman, as a 'wistful colloquy between two people'.[43] It precedes a solemn heralding that again suggests the funereal and the finalities in life and in relationships. The mournfulness lingers, then itself is terminated by a quivering crescendo of condolence that tails away with eddies from the harp into subdued grieving and thence into silence.

The third movement, the Rondo, marks a turning away from death and loss to vibrant life, but it does not offer the reassurance that might have been expected to balance and compensate for what has just gone before. From the outset the music is unsettled, then unsettling. It scurries hither and thither. Underscored heavily by the percussion, it moves into wildness and freneticism. There is a beating and a thudding, a hint of a demonic jack-in-the-box, then more manic acceleration and a conclusion that conveys a strong sense of the demented. Nowhere in the symphony are we more aware of the work as a succession of psychological states, some of them, like this one, extreme. In a letter to a friend Elgar related this passage of music to some lines in Tennyson's poem *Maud*, in which the hero, faced like Elgar with an impossible love, gives images of his suffering (one of which will figure in the similarly agonized words of Tiresias in T.S. Eliot's *The Waste Land*):

And my heart is a handful of dust,
And the wheels go over my head,
And my bones are shaken with pain.
For into a shallow grave they are thrust,
Only a yard beneath the street,
And the hoofs of the horses beat, beat,
The hoofs of the horses beat,
Beat into my scalp and my brain.

The Spirit of Delight stands apart from the tormenting rhythms of this world as, in the previous movement, it had from the apprehension of death.

How to come to terms with the extremes of painful feeling meticulously expressed in the second and third movements? Elgar believed that he had done this in the concluding Moderato and Maestoso. He told his publisher Alfred Littleton that 'the whole of the sorrow is soothed out and enabled in the last movement'.[44] Certainly it begins with a cheerful flowing melody. There is a sweeping lyricism confirmed by confident emphatic chords and continued by an unceasing buoyancy in the music. Some of the earlier themes associated with distress are heard again but transmuted in symphonic fashion by this new context. After these brief backward glances the suavely flowing confidence resumes. A triumphant beat emerges, the music now marching to a faster step than that heard in the Larghetto. There is a poignancy to the fragments of old themes as these are now again recollected. They fade and in so doing are assimilated into the thought-provoking coda, a slowly gathering crescendo of hushed gleaming strings.

Many listeners have found this ending to be more ambiguous than Elgar himself maintained. It is a thought-provoking, complex ending to a complex symphony. And this is undoubtedly one of the reasons that it did not enjoy the enthusiastic reception given to its predecessor, the First Symphony. Famously he found the first performance of the work at the Queen's Hall on 24 May 1911, with Elgar himself conducting, a bitter disappointment. At the end the response of the audience was subdued with none of the exuberant excitement that had followed the premiere of the First Symphony. Elgar was angry with his audience. To the leader of the orchestra, his friend W.H. Reed, he asked as he walked from the platform, 'What's the matter with them, Billy? They sit there like a lot of stuffed pigs.'[45]

A better and more understanding appreciation of the great, intricate art of this symphony lay with audiences to come. The year of the first performance, which saw the formal ending of the Edwardian Age with the coronation of King George V, was the moment when Elgar lost his brilliant, uncanny entente with audiences of his own generation and time. Within a very few years Britain was engaged in the First World War. After that cataclysm, which radically changed the social and cultural order in Britain, Elgar was seen as the composer of a past and very different generation. He lived for nearly a quarter of a century after the appearance of the Second Symphony, but during those years he lost that spark of inspiration that produced his finest work in the decade following the *Enigma Variations*.

After the Second Symphony he composed a good deal but nothing to approach the intensity and high art of that work – with one exception. He completed the Cello Concerto in the summer of 1919, just over six months after the Armistice had put an end to the unprecedented bloodletting and loss brought about by the Great War of 1914–18. It was a shocked, funereal time when just about every community in Britain – villages, towns and cities – was deliberating on the design of a memorial for its war dead. Elgar wrote the predominantly elegiac Cello Concerto in a burst of vitality and confidence that was rare for him at this time. At the end of June 1919 he told a friend, 'I am frantically busy writing and have nearly completed a Concerto for Violoncello – a real large work and I think *good* and alive.'[46]

The first performance was as much a setback for Elgar as that of the Second Symphony. The work was under-rehearsed and the playing by the London Symphony Orchestra poor. Today, however, it is recognized as one of the great works for the cello, exploiting to memorable effect the wide-ranging emotional and expressive possibilities that the instrument possesses. Elgar is especially successful in making its tenor voice sound out over and against the orchestra.

Fitting for the times, the Cello Concerto is a journey through tragic loss. For all that we hear in it, on occasion, the Elgar who could be the breezy Edwardian clubman, the piece is for the most part a keening, a lament. It is often seen, rightly, as an elegy for those lost in the terrible war that had just ended, but there is too a distinct personal edge to the music. It also sounds like a lament for the composer's own losses, perhaps his loss of audience, his loss of creativity, his loss, it may be, of Alice Stuart-Wortley.

The work begins rousingly, however, with sounds of defiance from the cellist, but these soon succumb to a long melody of world weariness. We hear yet again the Elgar of the *symboliste* generation. The orchestra enters offering endorsement and compassion for the solitary, sad voice. There is no symphonic challenging here. Encouraged, the cello soars as it explores its melancholy. Suddenly and brightly there comes an entry from the woodwind that quickens as even more rapturous understanding develops between the soloist and the tutti. Unhappiness is fully indulged and keenly investigated and then it falls away.

The second movement, Lento, begins in some uncertainty. Where to go from such an intense probing of loss? But then unexpectedly comes the Allegro molto, with its racing excitement and sheer joy expressed by the bravura cello. The Adagio, the shortest of the four movements, is a sharp recall, a *rappel à l'ordre*, a trenchant and unqualified acknowledgement of loss. The orchestra offers no debate whatsoever; players in the group simply offer overwhelming sympathy for the individual cello voice.

The Finale takes off quickly, the cello now performing a recitative. It is as though a mood of better spirits is being enforced. But the cello gradually becomes less confident. This time, however, the orchestra takes a different tack, continuing and encouraging the cheerfulness. The cello is persuaded and there is an ever-mounting accelerating excitement shared by the two. But there is such a thing as the ineluctable in life, something of which, emotionally speaking, the survivors of the Great War were destined to have a special experience. Painful yearning returns to the cello and the tutti accept the profoundly elegiac mood as the Adagio is reprised. The cello plays on grievingly, now slowing almost to a standstill. After the accompanied cadenza the sounds of defiance heard at the very beginning are heard again and the concluding bars of the concerto speed the work to a high-spirited triumphant conclusion that must strike the listener as something asserted rather than felt. In terms of Elgar's whole career it can sound like his last stand, his last act of defiance against the decline that he sensed within himself and saw in the society around him.

The two greatest composers who first and so spectacularly revitalized English music in the twentieth century, Edward Elgar and Ralph Vaughan Williams, saw very little of each other. One of their rare encounters, as we have seen, took place at the Three Choirs Festival in Hereford in the second week of September 1930, some ten years after the first performance of Elgar's Cello Concerto. It was a time of upset in both their lives, which mirrored and was in considerable part caused by the recent and very sudden turbulence that had destabilized the entire western world. Less than a year before their meeting there had occurred on 29 October 1929, Black Tuesday, the great stock market crash on Wall Street in New York. The economic, political and social consequences of this financial breakdown were to be calamitous for the North Atlantic countries throughout the coming decade. Germany was the country to be most drastically and devastatingly hit. Depression and rampant inflation swiftly intensified and extremist solutions from both the left and the right attracted strong support. A sign of what was to come was the result of the German election of 1930. Five days after the two English composers met, amidst the summer festivities of a cathedral city, Adolf Hitler's Nazi Party emerged, shockingly, as the second largest party in the Reichstag.

The Wall Street debacle had a speedy and marked effect upon the life of Sir Edward Elgar, OM, Master of the King's Music. With the contraction of the classical music industry in the aftermath of the slump, Elgar was forced to retrench drastically. During the ten years of King Edward VII's reign Elgar's career had been one of meteoric success. The oratorio *The Dream of Gerontius*, following on from the *Enigma Variations* of the preceding year, the widely popular *Pomp and Circumstance* marches of the following year and the ecstatically received First Symphony had brought him affluence as well as critical recognition and honours from the King. The itinerant provincial music teacher and regular commuter to Birmingham, who had had to struggle to make an income to support himself, was suddenly a man of means. He could afford to live in ever grander houses, including the imposing Severn House in Hampstead, designed by the prominent Victorian architect Norman Shaw. He could afford foreign travel and holidays abroad for himself and his family. He hobnobbed with very wealthy people. He dressed well and had his own personal manservant.

The financial crash of 1929 soon put an end to such luxury. Elgar had to give up his London flat in fashionable St James's; he also had to abandon his country house at Tiddington on the banks of the Avon near Stratford. He removed to a more modest house in his home city of Worcester: to Alice Stuart-Wortley, his correspondent of several decades, he depreciated it as 'a poor little place but a fitting end for a disastrous career – alas'.[47] To his old friend Adela Schuster he confided that, 'I must give up my little car and many other small comforts.'[48] He also let it be known that he was now prepared to sell the manuscripts of his early and historic compositions, but he found few takers. By 1930 his only composing projects were a piece for the Brass Band Composition Festival and an attempt to repeat his earlier successes with yet one more *Pomp and Circumstance March*, his fifth, which his publisher agreed to publish only grudgingly. Leslie Boosey reminded Elgar bluntly of their sales difficulties in the prevailing financial conditions, of 'the very serious falling off in the sale of the sheet copy'. Boosey noted pointedly that 'things are not what they were in the days when you wrote Pomp No. 1'.[49]

Elgar's financial misfortunes were accompanied by ill-health. Severe bronchitis in the spring of 1929 was followed by a painful and lengthy attack of sciatica. When he joined Vaughan Williams as one of the conductors at the 1930 Hereford Festival the seventy-three-year old Elgar had difficulty moving. When the time came for him to conduct his oratorio *The Apostles* he had to be helped up to the rostrum and could only conduct from a sitting position. Some four years later he was dead. And with his passing the first act of the dramatic revival of English music in modern times was at an end.

2

Ralph Vaughan Williams

A FTER ELGAR'S DEATH in 1934 Ralph Vaughan Williams was generally, and rightly, regarded as his successor as England's leading composer. Completing his Fourth Symphony in that year, the sixty-two-year-old Vaughan Williams had been a late developer in his musical career. During the Edwardian years, the decade of Elgar's heyday, Vaughan Williams was then in his thirties and beginning only very slowly to make his way in the world of music. It was not until 1910, the year of the premiere of Stravinsky's *Firebird* in Paris and when Elgar was at the pinnacle of his fame, that Vaughan Williams at last had his first major successes, with his immediately and lastingly admired *Fantasia on a Theme by Thomas Tallis* performed at the Three Choirs Festival in Gloucester on 6 September that year and with *A Sea Symphony* premiered five weeks later in Leeds Town Hall.

Vaughan Williams went on to receive increasing recognition for his achievements in a variety of musical forms. Individual songs such as 'Linden Lea' and 'Silent Noon' quickly became, and continue to be, popular favourites, as do some of his song cycles such as *On Wenlock Edge* and *Songs of Travel*. A number of his choral works, including *Dona nobis pacem* and *Sancta Civitas*, are still performed. And even more so some of his more popular works such as the Oboe Concerto and the overture to *The Wasps*. But for all his voluminous and varied output, it is his achievement in one particular genre of music that makes Vaughan Williams the leading composer of the twentieth century in England: his nine symphonies. Vaughan Williams is England's greatest symphonist. His work in this form is of a quality to make it part of the larger cultural consciousness of the time. His symphonies, viewed together, reveal a profundity that relates them to that of other major artists in the country during the century: Stanley Spencer, T.S. Eliot, D.H. Lawrence, Jacob Epstein and Henry Moore.

Vaughan Williams composed symphonies over a period of just short of half a century. And what tumultuous years they were! The first symphony predated the First World War; the ninth post-dated the Korean War. The nine works can readily be seen in part as responses to nine different phases of national experience as well as to distinctive stages in the life of the composer.

To trace the national story and the biographical story as these are related in the nine works is not to ignore the fact that they are, first and foremost, music. The nine symphonies are far more than, other than, narratives that can be translated into words. Music sounds what it means. And the semantics of music are of a very different form (and some, including the present writer, would say, a finer, more allusive form) from the semantics of words.

The essential paradox has been excellently formulated by Theodor Adorno:

> The fact that music, as language, imitates – that on the strength of its similarity to language it constantly poses a riddle, and yet, as non-signifying language, never answers it – must, nevertheless, not mislead us into erasing that element as a mere illusion. This quality of being a riddle, of saying something that the listener understands and yet does not understand, is something it shares with all art. No art can be pinned down as to what it says and yet it speaks.[50]

Vaughan Williams himself at times insisted that his work should be understood as pure music. He would resist attempts to give programmatic accounts of his symphonies. Yet in these, as well in many other of his major works, words are very much attached to the music. The first symphony, for instance, is a setting of passages of poetry by Walt Whitman. Words here have a partnership with music in the overall effect of the work. Each movement of the seventh symphony has a superscription referring the listener to texts: to sentences from the Old Testament, from the diaries of Captain Scott of the Antarctic and from the poetry of Shelley and Coleridge. For all his insistences that music was music and in no way expressive or referential, he was also ready to point to programmatic elements in his symphonies. Commenting on *A London Symphony* he even referred to specific streets and areas in the capital to which the different movements refer. Passages in the Ninth Symphony were, he noted, prompted by episodes in the narrative of *Tess of the D'Urbervilles* by the novelist he so deeply admired, Thomas Hardy. The final, elegiac passage of *A London Symphony* was, he told his friend Michael Kennedy, prompted by the concluding pages of a major work of Edwardian fiction, H.G. Wells's novel *Tono-Bungay*.

To attempt to describe Vaughan Williams's nine symphonies programmatically would lead to very dubious speculation and oversimplification. But to ignore his own allusions to their verbal and literary elements, intrinsic and extrinsic, would be to disregard clear indication of their relation to the composer's changing experience of living among the personal, social and political upheavals of the twentieth century. Vaughan Williams studied history at Cambridge in the 1890s and historical perspective was a conspicuous feature of his very lively writing about music throughout his life. It is very much there in the substantial essay he wrote at the end of the 1930s about Beethoven's Ninth Symphony. Early musical works such as the Thomas Tallis fantasia and his contributions to the *English Hymnal* show his keen concern with the history of music. It is appropriate then that his half century of symphonic writing should now be heard as a great work of history, history as it was experienced, most significantly as something heard and something reported auditorily. Taken together, the sequence of nine symphonies constitutes one of the greatest musical narratives produced in England in the twentieth century.

The story begins in October 1910 with the first performance of *A Sea Symphony*. This is very much an Edwardian artefact and of its time. It is difficult to imagine the work, with its confident, urgent optimism, appearing in any other period of musical history. To say why this is so requires some analysis and characterization of the word Edwardian. The near ten-year reign of King Edward VII is usually regarded as a distinct entity, something particular to itself and clearly distinct from the Victorian years that preceded it and the much-troubled reign of George V that followed. This is why the adjective has become established in common usage. But closer examination shows that the Edwardian period was far from being a chronological entity, politically, socially or culturally. The reign of King Edward VII was in fact very much a reign of two halves.

Half time was marked in January 1906, at the very centre of the decade, when the result of the general election was declared. It was one of the most momentous elections in British history. The Conservatives, who had been in power for more than ten years with Liberal Unionist support, suffered a landslide defeat and the Liberals formed a new government. With them in power a new mood of political and cultural optimism took over the country. Here is how, many years later, a historian characterized the second half of Edward VII's reign:

> These were the years of the greatest Liberal victory in English politics for a generation. The intellectual world responded to the optimism of the politicians. Here was the manifest triumph of that long nineteenth-century tradition of liberal humanism; the final defeat of obscurantism was at hand. It was one of those rare moments in history in which the atmosphere of life is lyrical and charged with hope, when man seems his own master, his destiny secure.[51]

The new government robustly set about a range of new social legislation that can now be seen as the foundation of the welfare state that was to be fully established by the middle of the century. Education was improved and extended for the poor and a pension system was created for those over seventy. A prominent member of this new, radical government was David Lloyd George, the fiery Welsh orator who was to prove to be the most influential political figure of the first quarter of the century. In April 1909, as Vaughan Williams worked on A Sea Symphony, Lloyd George, then Chancellor of the Exchequer, introduced a historic 'Peoples Budget', which was designed, he claimed, 'to wage implacable warfare against poverty and squalidness'. Certainly there could be no disputing that these were ugly aspects of Edwardian England, recorded in ample footage. However Lloyd George's introduction of land taxes as one means of finding money to assist those in poverty provoked violent opposition from the aristocrats (most of them wealthy landowners) who controlled the House of Lords. The upper house blocked Lloyd George's budget and a constitutional crisis ensued. The consequence was two general elections within the year of 1910 and the subsequent passing of the Parliament Act, which drastically reduced the powers of the aristocracy. It was one of the pivotal moments in the peaceful evolution of British democracy comparable to those of 1688 and 1832. This year of intense political turbulence was the context in which A Sea Symphony was completed and first performed. It was also the same year in which Elgar was completing his, at times, tortured Second Symphony. The profound uneasiness and uncertainties that recur in that work must surely, as

Jerrold Northrop Moore has suggested, have something to do with the Tory malaise at that time.

For Liberals and others who looked for a radically changed society in the future, the Parliament Act was a great victory. For progressives this was a heady, exciting moment. Their buoyant hopes for radical progress and a change in the human condition, together with a profound, even metaphysical belief in such change, inform Vaughan Williams's first symphonic statement. At this time he shared the visionary optimism of his great ancestors Josiah Wedgwood and Erasmus Darwin who, at some risk to themselves, subscribed to the principles of the French Revolution. It was a visionary optimism and a belief in democracy as the means to progress, which in the nineteenth century found no more eloquent voice than that of the great American poet Walt Whitman. Vaughan Williams had admired Whitman for some twenty years, after being introduced to his poetry by the future philosopher Bertrand Russell, his fellow student at Trinity College, Cambridge. *A Sea Symphony* was not his first setting of lines by the American poet. Almost three years to the day before the first performance of the symphony in Leeds, Vaughan Williams's setting for chorus and orchestra of lines by Whitman entitled *Toward the Unknown Region* had been performed at the same venue. The poem challenges the reader, or perhaps it is the poet's own inner being, to venture forth into unfamiliar areas of consciousness:

> Darest thou now O soul,
> Walk out with me toward the unknown region,
> Where neither ground is for the feet nor any path to follow?
> No map there, nor guide,
> Nor voice sounding, nor touch of human hand,
> Nor face with blooming flesh, nor lips, nor eyes, are in that land.

If such an act of adventurousness and courage is undertaken, then, Whitman concludes,

> Then we burst forth, we float,
> In Time and Space, O Soul, prepared for them.

Such radical vision also informs *A Sea Symphony* and some of the later symphonies. Vaughan Williams's admiration for Whitman lasted a lifetime.

In the very last month of his life he talked to Michael Kennedy about various literary enthusiasms which had 'gone off the boil' for him. 'And Whitman? I asked. "I've never got over him I'm glad to say," he replied.'[52]

Vaughan Williams was by no means alone in looking to Whitman for inspiration. Just a few years after the premiere of *A Sea Symphony* another great visionary artist, D.H. Lawrence, was to write:

Whitman the great poet has meant so much to me. Whitman, the one man breaking a way ahead. Whitman, the one pioneer. And only Whitman. No English pioneers, no French. No European pioneer poets. In Europe the would-be pioneers are mere innovators. The same in America. Ahead of Whitman, nothing. Ahead of all poets, pioneering into the wilderness of unopened life, Whitman. Beyond him, none. His wide, strange camp at the end of the great high-road. And lots of new little poets camping on Whitman's camping ground now. But none going really beyond. Because Whitman's camp is at the end of the road, and on the edge of a great precipice. Over the precipice, blue distances, and the blue hollow of the future.[53]

Lawrence later declares,

It is a great new doctrine. A doctrine of life. A new great morality. A morality of actual living, not of salvation … His was a morality of the soul living her life, not saving herself. Accepting the contact with other souls along the open way, as they live their lives. Never trying to save them … The soul living her life along the incarnate mystery of the open road.[54]

The last phrase inevitably brings to mind Vaughan Williams's often stirring song sequence of 1904, *Songs of Travel*, in which the phrase 'the open road' is a recurring motif. Robert Louis Stevenson, the poet who wrote the texts of the song cycle and one of those 'camping on Whitman's camping ground', had a qualified admiration for the American poet. But there can be no doubt that the Whitman sensibility pervasively affects these texts as it does the musical settings. For the progressives who felt that their hour had come with the general election of early 1906, Whitman had long been a support, a confirmation and an inspiration. One of the more prominent voices of democratic republicanism and anti-clericalism was that of the young A.C. Swinburne, whose poems Vaughan Williams was to set early on in his career. Swinburne's *To Walt Whitman in America* is a passionate homage of twenty-two seven-line stanzas addressed to his transatlantic contemporary. Some of the highly rhetorical verses prefigure the lines that Vaughan Williams would select for *A Sea Symphony*:

O strong-winged soul with prophetic
Lips hot with the bloodheats of song
With tremor of heartstrings magnetic,
With thoughts as thunders in throng
With consonant ardours of chords
That pierce men's souls as with swords
And hale them hearing along,

Make us too music, to be with us
As a word from a world's heart warm,
To sail the dark as a sea with us,
Full-sailed, outsinging the storm,
A song to put fire in our ears
Whose burning shall burn up tears,
Whose sign did battle reform;

A note in the ranks of a clarion,
A word in the wind of cheer,
To consume as with lightning the carrion
That makes time foul for us here;
In the air that our dead things infest
A blast of the breath of the west,
Till east way as west way is clear.

Out of the sun beyond sunset
From the evening whence morning shall be,
With the rollers in measureless onset
With the van of the storming sea,
With the world-wide wind, with the breath
That breaks ships driven upon death,
With the passion of all things free

For Vaughan Williams and his circle of gifted contemporaries at Cambridge, all of them staunch Liberals, Whitman's clarion calls served as an antidote to the melancholy, the world-weariness felt, or at least affected, by so many of the writers of the *fin de siècle,* the 1890s and the early years of Edward VII's reign. The poetry of Whitman, especially as it is integrated into vocal, choral and orchestral music in *A Sea Symphony,* establishes a feeling for and attitude to life that are vastly different from those in, for example, the Edwardian paintings by Walter Sickert and Joseph Conrad's two great works of Tory melancholy, *The Secret Agent* and *Nostromo.*

How unfamiliar and unexpected the great choral cries that open *A Sea Symphony* must have been to that first audience in Leeds in 1910! How different from the profound sadness and pessimism that are the chief subjects of Elgar's Violin Concerto and Second Symphony from around the same time. What opens *A Sea Symphony* is a great cry of excitement, joy – ecstasy even. The sea is greeted as an image of hope and endless possibility. In the light of later experiences Vaughan Williams's subsequent symphonies will at times be comparatively subdued, emotionally complex and increasingly subtle, sometimes to the detriment of a proper recognition and appreciation of their achievement. But not so his first symphony. Here is full-blooded exultation. As one critic has rightly noted, 'the dramatic shift from B flat minor to D major harmony at the word "sea" conjures a visceral sense of space opening up before us, and surely constitutes one of the great opening gestures of musical history.'[55]

The excitement flows on as the first movement proceeds to contemplate the ocean and the busy energetic movements of human beings and their ships on it. The particular and intense musical exhilaration in this opening imme-diately differentiates it from the several other works of this time that take up the subject of the sea, such as the orchestral suite *The Sea* by Frank Bridge, *The Oceanides* of Sibelius and Debussy's *La Mer.* At the end of the nineteenth century the sea was a topical subject. It presented a political issue. The expen-sive arms race that was then developing between Britain and Germany was primarily a matter of supremacy at sea, of ruling the waves, and that meant the number of battleships that each side possessed. The fate of nations was seen, as it never could be today, as something that would be settled by sea battles. The building of dreadnoughts, as the most advanced battleships were called, was a matter for urgent public concern and debate. The feeling of pride in Britain's naval strength and tradition throbs through Charles Villiers

Stanford's *Songs of the Fleet*. It is conspicuously there in the song 'The Little Admiral' with rousing first line, 'Stand by to reckon up your battleships'. To a greater or lesser extent it is there in all the poems by Henry Newbolt that supply the text for Stanford's sequence. Six years earlier Stanford had set similar Newbolt poems in his cycle *Songs of the Sea*. Both works catered very successfully to popular taste.

Songs of the Fleet premiered in 1910 at the same Leeds Festival as Vaughan Williams's *A Sea Symphony*. But musically and verbally, and in its attitude to experience, the younger man's work is vastly superior to the song sequence of his former teacher at the Royal College of Music in its early days in Kensington. Stanford's settings are parochial in their sound, subject and sentiment. Some of them are readily singable, but parochial nonetheless. From the outset of *A Sea Symphony* Vaughan Williams presents a music that calls to a wider humanity,

> a chant for the sailors of all nations
> Fitful, like a surge.
> Of sea-captains young and old, and the mates and of all intrepid sailors,
> Of the few, very choice, taciturn, who fate can never surprise nor death dismay

At that time of intensifying national rivalries and animosities Vaughan Williams's first movement concludes with a salute to a flag that flies over all human beings.

> A pennant universal, subtly waving all time, o'er all brave sailors,
> All seas, all ships.

These last four words constitute one of the several phrases subjected to repetition and permutation throughout this internationally minded movement. Such procedures are an important part of what Vaughan Williams understood as symphony at this stage of his career. As he told a journalist at the time,

> With regard to the name 'Symphony' – I use the word because the treatment of the words is symphonic rather than dramatic – that is to say the words are used as a basis on which to build up a decorative musical

67

scheme. I have therefore felt justified in repeating the words a good deal – especially in the 1st movement.[56]

Vaughan Williams was to have imposed on him a reputation as very much a national, and English, composer. Yet this first venture into symphonic form shows him to be very outward looking, to have a very American sense of human progress and a planetary awareness of the human condition. His choral and orchestral writing in this first symphony are based on a prosody, and especially a lineation, that were foreign to English poets of 1910. They generally found the Whitman line either outlandish or ludicrous. Only with the later arrival in British literary life of the American poets Ezra Pound and T.S. Eliot did prosody in England begin to change. As Michael Kennedy remarked, 'it is still a matter of wonder that Whitman's words have found music which fits them so naturally.'[57]

For Vaughan Williams *A Sea Symphony* was a matter of literary anthologizing as well as of musical setting. From the vast number of lines that constitute Whitman's *Leaves of Grass* and *Passage to India*, which was added to the 1871 edition of the former, he carefully selected passages that together would create a structure and a narrative and thematic unity. Words and music complementing each other present a progress in thought and feeling. In the second movement this progress becomes clearly apparent with the introduction of the first person pronoun underscored by the baritone voice. The symphony now shows itself to be built upon a balance between the inner consciousness of the 'I', which is the principal subject of the second and fourth movements, and the many and various wonders of the external world that are excitedly contemplated, revered and musicalized in the first and third movements.

The title of the second movement, 'On the Beach at Night, Alone' recalls that of a well-known poem by Matthew Arnold, *Dover Beach*. But the 'I' presented by Whitman and Vaughan Williams is very different from that of the troubled, alienated, even desperate consciousness speaking in Arnold's poem and prefiguring the melancholy that pervaded so much of European poetry in the later nineteenth century. The 'I' of *A Sea Symphony* has a view of a cosmos in which he is confident of his position.

> As I watch the bright stars shining,
>   I think a thought of the clef of the universe
>   and of the future.

A vast similitude interlocks all,
All distances of space however wide,
All distance of time
All souls, all living bodies though they be
      Ever so different.

The third movement, 'Scherzo – The Waves', turns away from the predominantly abstract words to express the sensuous power and charm of the world
of phenomenon well beyond the 'I'. Whitman's words inspire a beautiful
eddying, rippling music that suggests the displacement of the waves as a
'stately and rapid ship' passes through. Vaughan Williams's musical setting
delicately confirms the delight inspired by the movement of the waves.

    The final movement, entitled 'The Explorers', is by far the longest of the
four and, as is the usual custom in symphonic works, brings together and
reconciles the several opposites that have been presented in the previous
movements. But not before the nature of one of these, the 'I', has been further
explored and defined. The 'I' is now reformulated as yet another duality: self
and soul (a division that provided the subject and the title of a substantial
poem by W.B. Yeats). In Vaughan Williams's music there is the suggestion
of a love song, sung by the conscious verbal self to the spiritual self, 'thou
pressing me to thee, I thee to me, O soul', as, wooer-like, the brisk excited self
urges his spirit to set out on a life's adventure with him. Stirringly, resoundingly the choir hymns the soul as 'O, Thou transcendent!' Then the wooing
grows more urgent:

Away, O Soul! hoist instantly the anchor!
Cut the hawsers – haul out – shake out every sail!
Sail forth! steer for the deep waters only!
Reckless, O soul, exploring, I with thee, and thou with me.

The unity of being here envisaged is sounded again in the repetition of the
first five dramatically musicalized syllables that constitute some of the most
powerful bars in the symphony, 'O thou transcendent'.

    A music more acceptable to Edwardian taste is heard when the choir is
swept up into excited sea shanty rhythms as the 'I' orders the unprecedented
voyage into new areas of being and consciousness to begin. Thrilled expec-
tation was part of the intellectual climate of the first decade of the twentieth

century. Albert Einstein was reconfiguring notions of time and space. Aeroplanes were created. Liners crossed the Atlantic at ever increasing and competitive speeds. Exploration of unknown parts of the planet intensified as explorers were highly newsworthy. *A Sea Symphony* reverberates with this excited sense of new possibility. It is a great monument to late Edwardian optimism.

A London Symphony, Vaughan Williams's second symphonic work, was first performed in March 1914 on the eve of the outbreak of the First World War and, with the historical consonance that marks all of his symphonies, is an expression of the swift extinction of that hope and aspiration.

In an essay written at the time he was working on his second symphony Vaughan Williams resorts to the phrase 'the temper of the age'. It was a meaningful and important entity for him. Entitled 'Who Wants the English Composer?' and addressed to the readership of the *Royal College of Music Magazine*, the article is quick to accept that the English presently look abroad rather than to themselves for serious music. The notion of 'the land without music' still, in 1912, informs Vaughan Williams's words. But surely, he argues, England has the potential for a musical culture of its own. Beginning with a rhetorical question he proceeds to list some of the distinctive sounds in English life at that time that might provide the basis for such a culture (some of them do, in fact, appear in his second symphony):

> Have not we all about us forms of musical expression which we can take and purify and raise to the level of great art? For instance the lilt of a chorus at a music-hall joining in a popular song, the children dancing to a barrel organ, the rousing fervour of a Salvation Army hymn, St Paul's and a great choir singing in one of its festivals, the Welshmen striking up one of their own hymns whenever they win a goal at the international football match, the cries of street pedlars, the factory girls singing their sentimental songs? Have all these nothing to say to us?[58]

If the English composer fails to respond to such familiar, native things, then, Vaughan Williams argues, the consequence would be 'that he would lose one of the surest means of realising what he himself was dimly and inarticulately feeling and thinking, and that the temper of the age was in danger of passing over him, leaving him untouched and unready.'[59]

'The temper of the age', as it finds expression in *A London Symphony*, is one of sadness, melancholy, even elegy. The contrast with the preceding symphony is startling, dramatic. The reasons for the change can finally only be a matter for conjecture. Vaughan Williams's published letters from this time reveal little of his inner life; they deal for the most part with the practicalities of his increasingly successful career as a late-developing composer. But certainly the social and political climate to which he was always acutely sensitive had changed markedly in the three and a half years that separated the first performances of the two symphonies. The Liberal hopes and expectations of the latter Edwardian years, which he shared with his circle of progressive Cambridge friends, had to a great extent been achieved by the social and constitutional legislation put in place by the Liberal government of H.H. Asquith. But in the years just prior to the beginning of the First World War that same government had lost its progressive dynamic; it found itself pushed into a defensive, indeed conservative, position by the emergence of two powerful political forces. One was the energetic and sometimes violent campaign for votes for women. The second was a new stage in the divisive controversy, dating back many years, concerning Home Rule, or devolution, for Ireland. The notion of a predominantly Protestant Ulster being governed from Dublin produced the astonishing and shocking prospect of mutiny in the British army.

The campaign for women's right to vote entailed many instances of violent demonstration, terrorist sabotage and brutal imprisonment. An episode that shocked the world occurred when a suffragette, Emily Davidson, fatally threw herself under the King's horse at the Epsom Derby in June 1913. There is no evidence to suggest that either Vaughan Williams or his, by now ailing, wife took a strong interest in or a position on women's right to vote, but undoubtedly the sensational violence involved in the suffragettes' campaign would have disturbed that sense of unquestionable social decorum with which, as well-to-do Victorians, they had grown up.

On the burning issue of Irish Home Rule, which was similarly threatening the orthodoxies of British life, Vaughan Williams became more closely involved. In early August 1913 he made plans to go to Ireland on a cycling holiday with his much-admired friend from Cambridge days, Randolph Wedgwood. Apologizing for the age of his bicycle and his slow pedalling, the now forty-year-old Vaughan Williams arranged for them to meet at Waterford on 3 September. This proved to be just days after a police attack on a trade union rally in Dublin in which lives were lost. The episode is now recognized as one of the catalysts that brought about the Easter Rising in Dublin in April 1916. The two close friends, however, stayed away from Ireland's capital and cycled into the province of Munster and County Clare. Here they got into conversation, or perhaps an argument, with a 'gentleman of Killaloe'. Possibly without intending it, the two visitors were now confronted by one of the historic sites of Irish nationalism. Killaloe is a pretty village on the River Shannon with an ancient cathedral dating back to the thirteenth century; it is also the birthplace and an important location in the life of the great Irish hero of the eleventh century, Brian Boru. Liberating Ireland from what has been called the tyranny of the Norsemen, Brian Boru confirmed his standing as High King of Ireland by his historic victory at the Battle of Clontarf. An important and heroic figure for those who sought to heighten Irish conscious-ness and confidence at the beginning of the twentieth century, Brian Boru would certainly have been a subject of conversation when Vaughan Williams and his companion talked with the 'gentleman of Killaloe'. After Vaughan Williams's return to England his Irish acquaintance sent him a volume of Irish history. The composer's reaction to Ireland and to the dangerous political situation he found there was robust. Not only was he opposed to revolutionary change in Ireland, which at that time was still an integral part of Great Britain, he was also prepared to volunteer to fight to help prevent it. Vaughan Williams characteristically took public affairs very seriously and very much to heart throughout his life. The Irishman's gift of the history book, he told Randolph Wedgwood, 'makes me all the more prepared to volunteer (if they'll have me) on the side of law and order when the fight comes'.[60]

Ever responsive to 'the temper of the age', Vaughan Williams was like his fellow Liberal, Lloyd George, a firm believer in the British Empire and the range of 'law and order' that it represented. Now it was under threat he was prepared to take action on its behalf. He had been ready to support the Empire when it was challenged by the Boer War and now again he was eager when the future of its oldest component, Ireland, came into question.[61] But the man who had lived so long at the very centre of the imperial capital, in houses and streets just a stone's throw from the Houses of Parliament, Westminster Abbey and the grand pageantry associated with them, must surely have sensed that the social, political and psychological orthodoxies created by imperialism were now coming to an end.

In *A London Symphony*, in marked contrast to its predecessor, hope, confidence and exaltation are no longer the controlling feelings: far from it.

Now the supervening, controlling mood is one of reflection, melancholy and sadness as the composer ponders his city, which despite very audible moments of pleasure, excitement, pomp, drama and humour is heard as but a figment of time, gently alluded to by the chimes of Big Ben in the opening and concluding movements. Vaughan Williams's most revealing comments on this symphony appear in a letter he wrote to his friend and biographer Michael Kennedy in September 1957, referring him to the concluding paragraphs of *Tono-Bungay*, a substantial novel by the then highly renowned novelist H.G. Wells that was published in 1909, some five years prior to the first performance of *A London Symphony*. At the end of the book the narrator sails down the Thames and through London towards the sea. As night comes on and the bright lights of the imperial metropolis are gradually extinguished, 'Light after bright light goes down. England and the Kingdom, Britain and the Empire, the old prides and the old devotions glide abeam, astern, sink down upon the horizon, pass – pass. The river passes – London passes, England passes ...'

This destabilizing sense of the transitory nature of things, even something as substantial and vast as London, is at the heart of the symphony. The first movement may well gradually quicken from a dull early morning rumble into the sounds of urban bustle and purposefulness, and then end with a rousing finale conveying the excitement that city life can offer; however the second movement, Lento, develops with considered emphasis, a poignant sense of all things passing. A solo instrument recalls the blues just then beginning to be heard in London. There is then the melancholy of the Salvation Army playing in a street. From the middle of the nineteenth century, from the 'Tableaux parisiens' in Baudelaire's volume of poems *Les Fleurs du Mal*, writers, artists and composers had contemplated the sinister, ugly aspects of the exploding metropolis, the 'immonde cité'. *A London Symphony* belongs in this tradition. But it goes deeper than this. The heard mutations and ultimate transience of the city are but sound metaphors for the human condition itself. Towards the end of the second movement the programmatic references disappear into a grand, swelling funeral march. There is in this movement an extreme, almost unbearable tenderness and compassion for London and its noisy people, as they are contained within the larger process of transience.

The third movement, the Scherzo, brings some diversion from the tenderness. Cheerily we are returned for a comparatively brief period to the blaring of horns, to the scurry and hectic bustle of the streets of London. For this West End nocturne the listener should imagine himself, so Vaughan Williams recommends in his programme notes, 'on Westminster Embankment at night, surrounded by the distant sounds of The Strand, with its great hotels on one side, and the "New Cut" on the other, with its crowded streets and flaring lights.' But the glamorous excitements and rhythms of the London night inevitably fade away. The Scherzo ends with the last, slow flicker of late-night activity and, like the second and final movements, concludes by reaching into silence.

Vaughan Williams was to tinker with the score of the symphony over the years. The redaction confirmed in 1933 is the one usually played today and here the Scherzo and the final movement are both much shorter than in the first version of 1913. In that one, first recorded by Richard Hickox in 2001, the last two movements bring a much greater weight of melancholy to the work.[62] Vaughan Williams's friend Arnold Bax, to whom he would dedicate his Fourth Symphony, especially regretted 'the loss of a mysterious passage of strange and fascinating cacophony with which the first version of the *scherzo* closed'.[63]

The final movement remembers fleetingly the pulsing, drumming activity of the first. It also recalls, and resounds with, the music of London ceremonial and pomp. But then again comes the reminder of the passing of time from Big Ben. An eerily gloomy meditation follows and then at the last comes a conclusive sweep of melancholic resignation, with the final chord confirming a fade into nothingness. Vaughan Williams ends the symphony by conveying a sense of distance from human life, together with a sense of its ephemerality that only great artists are capable of. Certainly the living sounds of London life are there in the symphony, sometimes vividly so, but there also is the emptiness, the nothingness that are their context. It is a reality, a condition of human life that will be tellingly evoked again in the later symphonies, most notably the sixth, seventh and ninth.

From today's perspective the apocalyptic passages in *A London Symphony* seem prophetic, for within months of the first performance Europe was embroiled in the most destructive war in human history. Inevitably the First World War affected Vaughan Williams profoundly, especially as a symphonist.

At close to forty-two years of age in August 1914, Vaughan Williams was too old to be required to take part in the war. Nevertheless, with his strongly developed public spirit he was quick to volunteer. He served for the duration, initially in the Royal Army Medical Corps, and spent two periods close to the front line of the conflict. After training, in the company of young men some twenty years his junior, to obtain a commission, he was sent in March 1918 to join an artillery unit. When he arrived in France he found his unit to be in a forced retreat. One of his fellow officers remembered

> the retreat which began on March 21st, when the gun position was near Fontaine-les-Croiselles, some miles south of Arras and north of Bullecourt. We had retired twice and, when I first met Vaughan Williams, the guns were in position behind a wood, Athers Wood. I remember the guards passing us in open order with fixed bayonets. Vaughan Williams had not been with us for long and was in charge of the horse lines – not a 'cushy' job by any means.[64]

Before winning his commission Vaughan Williams had spent many months in the generally uneventful Salonika campaign against the Habsburg forces on the Greek-Bulgarian frontier. It must have been, at least at first, before he became extremely bored, a respite from the horrors he surely witnessed during his first period close to the trenches in northern France. This was at Ecoivres, a hamlet close to the River Somme and to the intense fighting and loss of life that took place in the summer of 1916, when Vaughan Williams was posted there as a medical orderly in the 2/4th London Field Ambulance. He described his duties in a letter to his close friend Gustav Holst, 'I am "Wagon orderly" and go up the line every day to bring back wounded and sick on a motor ambulance – this takes place at night – except an occasional day journey for urgent cases.'[65]

These experiences of the Great War were the origin of Vaughan Williams's next symphony, his third, given the misleading and unhelpful title *A Pastoral Symphony*. He clarified the sources and the nature of the symphony in a letter to his second wife, Ursula:

> It is really wartime music – a great deal of it incubated when I used to go up night after night in the ambulance wagon at Ecoivres and we went up a steep hill and there was a wonderful Corot-like landscape in the sunset – it's not really lambs frisking at all as most people take for granted.[66]

Today we can see this symphony as one of the major works of art deriving from the experience of front-line soldiers in the First World War. As a precipitate of that horrific episode in British history it belongs with the lyric poems of Wilfred Owen, the war paintings of Stanley Spencer, particularly those painted for the Sandham Memorial Chapel at Burghclere in Hampshire, and *In Parenthesis* by David Jones, which T.S. Eliot was quick to recognize as a masterpiece and to publish. The year of the symphony's premiere, 1922, also saw the publication of Eliot's *The Waste Land*, which, along with *Hugh Selwyn Mauberley* by Eliot's close friend and mentor Ezra Pound, is the major literary achievement in English literature deriving from the war and written by non-combatants. Vaughan Williams's third symphony is also, in one respect, about a waste land. It has rightly been called 'A dream of sad happiness – a requiem for Pan'. With its bugles, marches and a woman's keening lament, it is also a symphony about war, the war that laid waste the land.

Notoriously the initial responses to the work were not entirely positive. Philip Heseltine, who composed under the name Peter Warlock, mockingly commented that it was 'like a cow looking over a gate'. Even Ralph's long-standing friend and promoter Hugh Allen joked that, 'It suggested VW rolling over and over in a ploughed field on a wet day'. And Sir Thomas Beecham, as he finished conducting *A Pastoral Symphony*, is said to have laid down his baton and confided to his orchestra players, 'A city life for me, then'. Certainly the third symphony, in its ironic evocation of a pastoral world, is less arresting, less immediately compelling than the evocation of the ocean in *A Sea Symphony* and of city life in *A London Symphony*. For long stretches it is more laid-back, more understated than either of its predecessors. But as we continue to listen to it we become aware, as we do in that highly auditory prose poem *In Parenthesis,* of its richness of implication, subtlety and restraint. The influence of Ravel, with whom Ralph had spent time studying six years before the outbreak of the Great War, is very audible in the symphony.

The first movement, Molto moderato, like the second and the fourth, is one of long lingering melancholy and mournfulness. But in this opening such emotions are infiltrated, carried along by, and then assimilated into a rather English, quick-flowing cheeriness. This is eventually swept aside by a swiftly strengthening and more textured lyrical impulse that contains within in something that is characteristic of Vaughan Williams, a complex of deeply felt emotions. Here they are feelings of loss, pride and sadness; at a deep level they underlie the symphony as a whole.

The second movement, the dark-toned, nocturnal Lento moderato, establishes with unmistakable audibility that Ralph's pastoral world is a distorted version of that in Beethoven's Sixth Symphony, with which Vaughan

Williams's title clearly prompts comparison. In T.S. Eliot's landscape of the First World War, *The Waste Land*, published in the same year as the premiere of *A Pastoral Symphony*, the allusions to the music of Wagner create a similarly painful contrast. Vaughan Williams's pastoral landscape is by no means that of Beethoven, nor of his contemporary Wordsworth – nor even that of the less vital, more sentimental nature Romantics whose poems appeared in the series of anthologies, *Georgian Poetry*, that Winston Churchill's secretary, Edward Marsh, began publishing just before the Great War. Vaughan Williams's symphony explores the experience, the feelings of pastoral lost. An outstanding and memorable sound in the work is a cadenza for natural trumpet, which brings to our ears the distinctive sound of the First World War in the fields of northern France, the army bugles sounding out at nightfall over no-man's land and the trenches. It was a sound that Vaughan Williams long remembered after his time as an ambulance orderly in Ecoivres.

George Butterworth, the young friend who shared Vaughan Williams's enthusiasm for collecting folk songs and dances, had been an important influence in persuading Vaughan Williams to write the symphony. It makes the haunting bugle sound all the more poignant for the listener, and surely for Vaughan Williams himself, to recall that it was at Pozières, during the Battle of the Somme, that the composer of the idyll *The Banks of Green Willow* was shot through the head by a sniper.

The third movement, Moderato pesante, interrupts the mournful meditation with the fragmented uproar of a scherzo. Heartiness fleetingly enters into the music. We hear the brassiness of a regimental march or of a soldiers' marching song or folk song. But that is far from being the final word about the devastation that is the subject of the symphony. The final movement, Lento, brings another contrast and surprise, a woman's voice wordlessly keening. After this elemental human sound there comes from the orchestra a solemn hymn for the dead – and then a panicky, stricken dialogue between the strings and woodwind. Closure has not come. And then chillingly the keening soprano returns. The symphony ends with what sounds like a very ancient primitive response to the terrible losses in this modern war.

By no means all of those who heard the first performance of the symphony in January 1922, played by the Orchestra of the Royal Philharmonic Society, were lukewarm or confused in their responses. Three days after the premiere Lucy Broadwood, Vaughan Williams's long-standing colleague in the folk-song movement, wrote to him exuberantly, 'Thank you a million times for the gorgeously beautiful symphony you gave us … The trumpet stirred me desperately – and how finely it was played.' She hoped that Ralph was pleased by the excited response of the audience and of the players in the orchestra. She was also surely aware of how this new symphony sounded athwart the Beethoven work that Vaughan Williams's title brought to mind: 'I hope that some of our joy returned, reflected, to you and that the "Old Philharmonic" shouting and waving to you across the dour bust of Beethoven was a happy thing, and a funny thing too, for you.'[67]

More than thirteen years were to pass before Vaughan Williams's next symphony, his fourth, received its first performance. During this period he wrote a good deal of music in other genres. In two of them, *Sancta civitas*, first performed three years after *A Pastoral Symphony*, and *Job*, premiered some four years later, the thematic seriousness, care for structure and detailed musical patterning that characterize the symphony as a form are prominent, even assertive. Vaughan Williams called *Sancta civitas* an oratorio and certainly the vocal passages for soloists and chorus are, in relation to the orchestral score, more central and important than those in *A Sea Symphony*. Perhaps more than any other of his major works *Sancta civitas* has a very intimate connection with the historical moment in which it appeared. When he won the general election in December 1918 Lloyd George had promised the returning soldiers 'a country fit for heroes to live in'. By 1926 this Wagnerian promise was proving to be false. In the worsening economic and financial crisis of the mid-1920s the colliery owners of Great Britain bluntly informed the miners, a number of whom were former soldiers, that they would have to accept a substantial reduction in their wages. Coal was at that time the chief energy source of the nation. The functioning of society depended on it. Not for the last time in the twentieth century this crucial industry was in a crisis that had national implications. The miners refused to accept the proprietors' diktat and, under the leadership of their eloquent and left-wing union leader A.J. Cook, they soon began a nationwide strike. When the owners responded by locking them out, the Trade Union Congress resolved to take the momentous step of calling on other unions to join a General Strike in support of the miners. It began at a minute before midnight on 3 May 1936. *Sancta civitas* had its premiere in Oxford on the fourth day of the General Strike.

The composer's near contemporary, Winston Churchill, now Chancellor of the Exchequer, feared and vigorously warned that this total disruption to everyday life could well be a prelude to a communist revolution such as had happened in Russia less than ten years before. He proposed putting tanks and machine guns onto the streets to protect strike-breaking food convoys. The Prime Minister, the more moderate Stanley Baldwin, argued for greater caution. To deflect Churchill's reactionary energies Baldwin made him responsible for the government newspaper, the *British Gazette*, which together with the TUC's *British Worker* was the only press to appear during the national shutdown. The headline over the central column in Churchill's *British Gazette* of 5 May encapsulated in a phrase what he saw as the stark choice: 'The Constitution or a Soviet'.

Two days later the army was ordered onto the streets to escort the lorries that were forcing their way through the dockers' picket lines in the East End to bring food into the capital. At the same time artillery pieces and barbed-wire entrenchments appeared in Hyde Park. In north-east England an express train drawn by the record-breaking *Flying Scotsman* was derailed by strikers.

As Ursula Vaughan Williams reported in her biography of her husband, he was 'deeply troubled' by the violent crisis dividing the nation. As we have seen, he was always ready to step forward and involve himself in public affairs. To settle his conflicting thoughts and try to decide what he would do if the country were to fall into revolution and class war, he made the effort to detail his complicated, ambivalent attitude to the General Strike in a page and a half, beginning 'On the whole I am with the miners in this dispute.' He mistrusted Churchill and his 'gang in the cabinet; and 'the beastly rag the National (sic) Gazette which is trying to inflame evil passions is theirs also.' He then went on to ask himself directly, 'isn't it our duty to support the gov't as such even if in the end it has to resort to armed force?' Then he put the same question in another way: 'is it wrong to be on the side of revolution if it came to that?' At this stage in his conflicted meditation he decided that 'I should not be against revolution by violence in the last resort (I don't think the status quo anything to be proud of).'

But immediately an important proviso came into his mind. Before envis-aging 'the temporary anarchy which would follow I must be certain that a *better* state of things is going to emerge.' And this he doubted. 'Much as I dislike the govt I mistrust the labour leaders ... Cook is an empty windbag.' Another simple fact gave him pause too: 'Also I cannot deny the duty of the govt to see that people do not starve if the food is to be had.' The problem was frustratingly unsolvable: 'The simplest thing for a man of my age is to do nothing.' But to a man of his temperament and readiness for action such an abdication was painfully unsatisfactory too. He continued to meditate about the issue without finally coming to any resolution.

He was struggling with these questions and writing out his position paper while he and his first wife Adeline were staying in Oxford with her brother, the historian H.A.L. Fisher, formerly a Lloyd George cabinet minister and now Warden of New College. Doubtless the national crisis was the subject of intense discussion during the visit. Vaughan Williams was in Oxford to attend the concluding rehearsals and the first performance of his oratorio *Sancta Civitas*, which took place the day before the government used troops to effect entry into the London docks. The work was a composition born of the hopes so deeply cherished by those returning from the horrific war. What an irony that Vaughan Williams's musical evocation of the coming of a *sancta civitas*, a holy city, a divine polity should be first heard at such a dangerous, potentially violent and brutal moment.

The oratorio is about the Apocalypse and is a setting of a selection of passages from Revelation, the final book of the New Testament. In the aftermath of the horrors of the First World War and among the dizzying dislocations, financial, economic and social, that subsequently ravaged Europe, a sense of approaching apocalypse informed a number of the major artistic enterprises of the time. It is conspicuously there, for instance, in W.B. Yeats's poems of this period and in T.S. Eliot's *The Waste Land*. It is also present in D.H. Lawrence's novel *Women in Love*, which in one redaction took its title from the *Dies Irae*, the thirteenth-century Latin hymn about the Apocalypse, the Day of Judgement. It is characteristic of Vaughan Williams's literary and linguistic sophistication that when he too turned to this imposing visionary subject he selected his texts not only from the King James version of the Bible but also from the earlier version by Richard Taverner (1539), which is marked by a lexical preference for the Anglo Saxon, the concrete and the earthy rather than the Latinate.

The passages that Vaughan Williams collaged present a vision of devastation followed by one of human, planetary and cosmic salvation. The epigraph on the first page of the score endorses the ambitiousness, the great scale of the project. The words are taken from Plato's *Phaedo* and they deflect the listener's thoughts from the Bible to this other, non-Christian text, which enlarges the work's frame of reference yet also confirms the existence, durability and ultimate triumph of an entity that can be termed the spiritual. Vaughan Williams's copy of F.J. Church's translation from Plato's Greek is heavily marked:

> A man of sense will not insist that things are exactly as I have described them. But I think he will believe that something of the kind is true of the soul and her habitations ... The venture is a fair one and he must charm his doubts with spells like these.

Doubts! Spells! The work is Vaughan Williams's struggle to sideline his agnostic doubts and to achieve a vision of redemption from destruction. It is a subject that befits symphonic form and the oratorio can be seen to fall into four sections that are strongly reminiscent of symphonic structure.

At the start of the work the auditory vision emerges from silence, cellos and basses mounting a slow, rising progression. Into this music of mystery enters the voice of the protagonist, John of Patmos, declaiming the imminent marriage of Jesus, the Lamb of God, to his people. Distant, then ever nearer, the choral voice of humanity joins and is recruited to him.

In the second section of *Sancta Civitas* there develops a complex sequence of metaphors. The divine figure mutates from the Lamb to the warrior, Faithful and True, astride a white horse. Introduced by urgent drumming, this warrior figure makes war against the kings of the earth and destroys them. We now hear military music. The fieriness of the conqueror is expressed in a powerful triple forte chord of G minor and then follows a passage of disturbing ferocity and brutality.

The third section is in marked contrast. The urgently martial and then victorious sounds are suddenly replaced by slower, more lingering ones. These are the sounds of regret and of loss. Babylon has been destroyed but the music puts us into two minds about its obliteration and the loss of all its 'things that were dainty and goodly'. The recent war of 1914–18 may have been won but the destruction that the victory has cost is also an occasion for sadness. We have here, as Michael Kennedy observed, 'masterly pages of choral writing like a vast symphonic sigh'.[68] The sounds of *Sancta Civitas* do not constitute a simple vision. Along the journey to a perception of redemption there is ambiguity and doubt.

Finally, in the fourth section, Vaughan Williams delicately musicalizes the slowly dawning prospect of a sancta civitas. A solo violin hauntingly develops the hushed vision. Then a trumpet announces the 'Holy, Holy, Holy' and the music takes on a growing urgency and compelling emphasis. It culminates most dramatically in a highly memorable understatement from the tenor soloist. This is, in three short sentences, the simple, quiet declaration from the Redeemer: 'Behold I come quickly. I am the bright and morning star. Surely I come quickly.' This still, quiet vocal entrance has immediate power. Almost a quiet afterthought following the orchestral music preceding, these short, sung sentences have a profound effect on audiences by bringing simple, unambiguous reassurance. And then the conclusion of the vision after these quickening, highly affecting words is a trailing away into the quietness and then the silence in which the powerful, complex vision of salvation and redemption first developed.

～

A year after the first performance of *Sancta Civitas* Vaughan Williams undertook a subject of similar profundity. This resulted in *Job, A Masque for Dancing*. Listening to the music Vaughan Williams composed, an audience might not readily recognize this as a work for dancers. At times it sounds like a concerto for orchestra comparable in its particular texture to those of Bartók and Lutosławski. But unquestionably its length, scope, structure, patterning, detailing and dialectical progress also give what is ostensibly dance music the characteristics of a symphony.

Work on the piece originated in 1927, which was the hundredth anniversary of the death of William Blake. The subject of Job was very much in keeping with these times of economic depression and deprivation. Geoffrey Keynes, a Blake scholar, surgeon and balletomane, set out to commemorate the centennial by creating a ballet based on Blake's *Illustrations of the Book of Job*. Keynes wrote a scenario relating the story of Job's life and trials. He then turned to his wife's sister, the artist Gwen Raverat (the author of a fine memoir, *Period Piece*, which offers glimpses of Vaughan Williams as an undergraduate at Cambridge), to design the stage sets. It was very much a Cambridge enterprise. Geoffrey Keynes's brother, the Cambridge economist John Maynard Keynes, was one of those who agreed to help with the financing of the masque. The project was also supported by the Camargo Society, an important new organization in the history of the art of dance in Britain. During the 1920s the Camargo Society sought to stabilize and promote ballet in London by mounting productions that employed dancers from the Marie Rambert and Ninette de Valois dance companies. A very active member of Camargo was the idealistic and campaigning music critic Edwin Evans, Vaughan Williams's advocate from years before. Very likely at Evans's suggestion Geoffrey Keynes invited Vaughan Williams to write the music for *Job*. The composer was quickly inspired by the subject. He spent hours in discussion of the project with his long-standing friend Gustav Holst. Years later Vaughan Williams acknowledged, 'I owe the life of *Job* to Holst.'[69]

Geoffrey Keynes decided to submit the work to Serge Diaghilev, whose renowned Ballets Russes had now removed from Paris to Monte Carlo, but the pre-eminent dance impresario of the day rejected *Job* for being 'too English' and 'too old-fashioned'. However, Vaughan Williams was not greatly discouraged by this rejection. Writing to his collaborator and distant relation Gwen Raverat, he commented:

> I never expected Djag (*sic*) wd look at it – & I'm glad on the whole – the 'reclame' would have been rather amusing – but it wdnt have suited the sham serious really decadent & frivolous attitude of the R.B. [Russian Ballet] toward everything – can you imagine Job sandwiched between 'Les Biches' & 'Cimarosiana' – & that dreadful cultured audience saying to each other 'My dear, have you seen God at the Russian ballet?' No – I think we are well out of it.[70]

Despite Diaghilev's rejection, Vaughan Williams proceeded with the orchestral rehearsals of the piece. At each session he was assisted by Gustav Holst in finalizing what had become a very substantial, intricate composition.

In October 1930 *Job* had its first performance at Norwich as a concert piece, which it still continues to be. In the following February Vaughan Williams conducted a performance from the original studios of the BBC on Savoy Hill. Only in July 1931 did the Camargo Society give the first stage performance, at the Cambridge Theatre, London. The sometime Ballets Russes dancer Anton Dolin danced the role of Satan and the young Constant Lambert conducted the orchestra. The choreography was by Ninette de Valois. The first public stage performance of *Job* took place later in the year at the Old Vic, where there would be further performances until 1932. Among the many admirers of the work was the young Ursula Lock, who was at that time studying acting at the Old Vic. Six years later she would become the composer's lover.

Job, A Masque for Dancing is made up of nine scenes and is essentially a narrative, but there is far more to it than that. It contains musical themes that are subtly developed and interwoven. It also offers memorable orchestral effects and colouring with striking passages for individual instruments, some of them (the xylophone and the tenor saxophone, for instance) still unusual in concert orchestras at the end of the 1920s. The overall soundscape is given a complex design that brings before the listener, in sounds as well as in the words identifying the scenes, philosophical, metaphysical and religious issues. In this work, as in *Sancta Civitas*, we see, and above all hear, Vaughan Williams delving far deeper into the human condition than in his first two symphonies. In these two pieces from the 1920s he employs essentially symphonic form as a means of understanding and assimilating the horrendous destruction of human lives and human condition brought about by the First World War.

Following the Old Testament narrative, *Job* begins with an introductory movement in which slow, steady orchestral rhythms and then rustic passages for flute and violin evoke the initial wellbeing of the patriarch Job and his family. The setting and the mood are pastoral. Then comes a dramatic disturbance. This is the second theme, which will recur in various permutations throughout the work. Violent descending octaves on strings and bassoon introduce the Satan figure, which will seek to disrupt and destroy the human contentment presented earlier. Then comes another contrasting theme, the 'Saraband of the Sons of God', a movement that announces the existence of a countervailing power; it is music that has a beautiful and reassuring stateliness.

But then, very much in symphonic manner, Satan returns, more forcefully and aggressively than before. 'Satan's Dance of Triumph' is made up of mocking yet menacing sounds, prominent among them the raucous, irreverent clatter of the xylophone. It then moves on to a magnificently vainglorious climax in an *alla marcia* driven by blaring trombones.

The third scene of the masque is a dance movement, the 'Minuet of the Sons of Job and their Wives'. The courtly dance reveals the assured, elegant complacency of the young things who are the beneficiaries and inheritors of the Job patrimony. But their gracious living is slowly undermined, then violently racked by the shrill, destructive discords that are the sounds of Satan. The fourth scene, entitled 'Job's Dream', brings us to the very middle of the narrative and to a climax in the developing conflict of musical themes. Here there is heard the very nadir of Job's downfall, his sense of material, psychological and spiritual dispossession. He loses his affluence, his family and, as a result of his loss of belief and trust in God, his own selfhood. The thudding pizzicato and the frenetic 1920s jazz sounds give us Job's dizzying panic and extreme mental disorder.

The fifth scene begins the second half of the work, the journey back, the journey to redemption. Here a delicate cantabile melody for the first violin emerges from the heavy, throbbing stultifying percussion to offer a tenuous reassurance and a glimpse of hope. The sixth scene reveals a failure to develop this restorative awareness; here comes the music of self-pity, with blues-style whining on the saxophone. But this in turn is swept away by the thundering of the Almighty, which resonates in the dominating organ sound. The human voice of redemption introduces itself in the seventh scene, 'Elihu's Dance of Youth and Beauty'. Job is here reassured by his neighbour Elihu in a lyrical, then increasingly excited and finally ecstatic violin solo. The Satan theme attempts one more entrance, only to be swept away by God in music of calm command. Then, again in the way of symphonic procedure, the themes voiced in terrestrial sounds complement and meld with those of the divine. The 'Galliard of the Sons of the Morning' is an assured and stately music of triumph that is in no way triumphalist. The penultimate scene, 'Altar Dance and Heavenly Pavane', an allegretto of accelerating joyousness and content-ment, culminates in one last surge of restored human happiness.

The final scene takes us back to the quiet, steady contentment eroded in the first movement of the masque. The effect of this return is thematically dramatic. It is no less than a subtle intimation of the eternal. It is a fine example of Vaughan Williams's profound, albeit laid-back ambitiousness as an artist. The first and last movements create a frame that contains and ultimately supervenes man's struggle with the Satanic and the destructive. Before, after and (the musical structure of *Job* implies) above human doubt, despair and conflict there can be heard the soundings of another reality. That he should take on such a subject is one of the indications of the stature of Vaughan Williams as a composer.

~

In 1931, the year after *Job* was first performed, Vaughan Williams began writing his Fourth Symphony. The music here is an astonishing contrast to all that has gone before in his career. It begins with what is still today a shocking explosion of violence and anger. The same strident, pounding sounds of frustration and destructiveness are to be heard in the opening toccata of his unjustly neglected Piano Concerto, which was written around the same time. Is such, for him, entirely unprecedented music a representation of a personal mood, as Vaughan Williams himself once suggested, or of a social and political situation, as critics and historians have often suggested? Or of all of these? This seems most likely. Ursula Vaughan Williams also emphasized how closely this symphony is related to the character of the man who wrote it: 'the towering furies of which he was capable, his fire, pride and strength are all revealed'. She also adds, illuminatingly, that 'The Symphony has something in common with one of Rembrandt's self-portraits in middle age.'

But why, the listener must wonder, did he, as he approached the age of sixty, give vent to this aspect of himself? Certainly there were a succession of painful blows in his personal life at the time. The death in 1934 of his closest friend and colleague Gustav Holst was a great loss. He also learned that his wife Adeline's painful arthritis and ever-increasing debilitation could never be cured. Her condition was the prime reason for giving up the house in Cheyne Walk, Chelsea, and buying, in May 1933, The White Gates, a house on the outskirts of Dorking, close to the Surrey countryside. It is very much to be doubted whether Vaughan Williams was ever as happy as a commuter to London, as he now was, than he was in earlier and later years as a resident of the capital city.

For a man as concerned as he was with social and political issues, the Depression that destabilized all the North Atlantic countries after the financial crash on Wall Street in 1929 must have been demoralizing. A world fit for the heroes with whom he had served had not come to pass. Also, as Vaughan Williams worked at this symphony, a defeated Germany was both resurgent and a cause of concern. In March 1933 an Enabling Act in the German Reichstag granted Adolf Hitler the powers of a dictator. Nazi policies were rapidly brought into law during that spring and summer. In April Julius Streicher, the editor of the Nazi newspaper *Der Stürmer* and publisher of anti-Semitic books for children, organized a nationwide boycott of Jewish businesses. The following month, in just about every German city and university town, the Nazis organized public burnings of thousands of books they considered decadent.

In such a time of upheaval, the Fourth Symphony was composed. An early mention of it comes in 1931 when Vaughan Williams, long labelled as a traditionalist and a romantic, spoke of writing a symphony in response to the music heard at what he disparagingly described as the 'Freak Festivals' organized by the International Society for Contemporary Music. This was the organization dedicated to the promotion of the music of innovative composers such as Schoenberg, Webern, Berg and Bartók. Early in his career Benjamin Britten was a regular attender at the ISCM's music festivals. Vaughan Williams was very ready to scorn this music, but with the Fourth Symphony he reveals himself as a closet modernist. He was by now clearly susceptible to the Modernist idiom and here it has clearly affected and infiltrated his composing. Probably to Vaughan Williams's dismay, his close friend Gustav Holst heard an early piano version and did not like it. Vaughan Williams, however, persevered with his startlingly innovative piece, though not with total confidence. Six months before its first performance he was writing uneasily to its proposed conductor, Adrian Boult, 'I want you to hear the Symph on 2 pianos <u>soon</u> because I want to get down to it and wash its face ...'[71] His staunchest and closest musical adviser, his wife Adeline, also had doubts about the work, right up to the last minute. Just two days before Adrian Boult premiered the piece she wrote to her sister, 'Beloved Boo', about her vacillating attitude to the astonishing work: 'The symph is emerging and now I couldn't bear you not to hear it. Last week I thought I couldn't bear anyone to hear it! It was wonderful to get the first movement going this morning – it's powerful – I ought to have had more faith.'[72]

Adeline's ambivalence is understandable. How taken aback those listeners in April 1935 must have been by that first movement! The violence of the anger is still shocking today. Nowhere among the many extant recordings of the symphony is the anger more strongly brought out and emphasized than in the version Vaughan Williams himself recorded with the London Symphony Orchestra in October 1937. Anger, even bitterness, is the premise, the point of departure of the symphony. The remainder of the work can be seen as a series of attempts to come to terms with the shattering outburst that begins the piece.

The braying, thundering percussive chords that open the work are succeeded by a second subject, a gently flowing meditative theme that occasionally sounds jagged and disrupted. This is especially so under the baton of Vaughan Williams (other conductors typically bring out the gentleness here far more than he does). The second theme, at times sounding lost and lonely as it wanders on, concludes with a controlled, subdued memory of the thunderous agitation of the start. There is then a falling away into quietness, all violence spent. The contrast between the beginning and the end of the movement is a dramatic one. The shock of incontinent violence is at the last, at least temporarily, assimilated.

The second movement, Andante moderato, brings the sound of the pondering of someone undergoing an emotional hangover. It begins with slow reflections that lead to a gently pulsing lyrical theme intimating revival and renewal after exhaustion. A first percussive climax shows some confidence achieved. But then follows a return to somewhat forlorn meandering with intricately patterned tensions and dissonant counterpoint. The wandering ends with another form of consolation, the melancholy compassionate lament of the flute that tapers off into silence. The third movement, Scherzo, barges in, intrusively hearty; this is 'wake up, pull yourself together' music that joshes along, noisily jokey. There is just one pause, a moment of quiet thoughtfulness that is swiftly brushed aside by an 'oompah' beat and a march tune from the woodwind.

However the rending anger and underlying violence that are the recurring concerns of this symphony cannot be put aside by a resorting to cheeriness and hearty humour. The explosive anger sweeps up again at the beginning of the final movement and seethes. It may briefly decelerate to a more bustling irritation and even to some moments of meditation. but these are quickly ended and the violence, psychological or social, regathers and builds to an alarming knockabout climax. In the fugal epilogue it intensifies still further and reaches boiling point. It concludes with a final chord that is contemptuous, aggressive and unanswerable. Listeners are left in shock and silence. The concluding bars of this powerful symphony are as violently disturbed as those at the very beginning. Destructive turmoil has been experienced; it has been allowed its course, considered and attempts have been made to contain it. But at the last it has triumphantly returned to overrun the conclusion and to end the symphony with one final brutal detonation.

The work is a presentation and a consideration of destructiveness in life. It is the very same subject that T.S. Eliot was to address memorably in 'The Dry Salvages' from his *Four Quartets*, published just six years after the first public performance of the Fourth Symphony. At the end of the second movement of this 'quartet' Eliot writes of 'the ragged rock in the restless waters' of life, which:

In the sombre season
Or the sudden fury, is what it always was.

Vaughan Williams, as has been reported, was himself a man very capable of 'sudden fury' and he wrote this symphony in a decade and within a continent where such atavism disastrously affected human life. It was not, of course, a work of such conscious, explicit intention. As Vaughan Williams told his friend Robert Longman,

> I wrote it not as a definite picture of anything external e.g. the state of Europe – but simply because it occurred to me like this – I can't explain why – I didn't think that sitting down and thinking about great things ever produced a great work of art ... A thing just comes – or it doesn't – usually doesn't – I always live in hope, as all writers must, that one day I shall 'ring the bell'.[73]

For all its outlandish innovations, the Fourth Symphony quickly had many admirers. They found that it sounded of the times. The composer Arthur Benjamin, for instance, wrote to Vaughan Williams:

> I write to tell you how deeply moved I was with your new Symphony, how much I admired its sheer mastery, its vitality and beauty ... To me it is the crystallisation of all that contemporary composers have been *trying* to do and, as much as I admire Sibelius, I find him tentative in comparison to you. It was a joy to hear the public so spontaneously enthusiastic and so genuinely carried away.[74]

Another young composer, Edmund Rubbra, wrote to Vaughan Williams of the work's 'almost overwhelming power and beauty'. An old friend and colleague from the English Folk Dance and Song Society, Maud Karpeles, found the symphony 'tremendous' and tried hard to define

> what it conveyed to me – the feeling of some huge force driving us to fight and struggle, which may eventually shatter us to pieces. And yet we know in our hearts that there is something in life which withstands destruction and brings order out of disorder and the secret of it is to be found in music and particularly in your music.[75]

That redemptive 'something in life' to which Maud Karpeles refers is far less available in the Fourth Symphony than in the three earlier ones. Perhaps it is to them or to his work as a whole to date to which she refers, for the concluding bars of the Fourth Symphony are far from orderly. The final, thumping chord can sound like a provocation, perhaps even an insult to the audience. It shares something of the contempt and bitterness expressed in a famous poem of, and characterizing, the 1930s, W.H. Auden's 'September 1939', in which the writer scornfully ponders a 'low, dishonest decade'.

The attitude to the audience in Vaughan Williams's next symphony, and indeed the overall feeling expressed in the piece, are altogether different. The music now is consolatory; it invites to a secular communion. The great attitudinal range of Vaughan Williams's symphonies here gains a further and distinctive extension.

The Fifth Symphony was produced during the Second World War for an audience that by 1943 was war-weary. As such it is radically different from its successor, the Sixth Symphony, which is a retrospective, distanced consideration of the emotional aftershocks of the horrors and enormities that were particular to the Second World War. Within the overall context of Vaughan Williams's symphonic sequence and of its reading of his times, the Sixth stands revealingly and allusively as a contrast to the *Pastoral Symphony*, which is his retrospective consideration of the First World War, a conflict which in its nature and in its effect upon him was entirely different from the Second.

The Fifth Symphony, then, is the first of two to be inspired by the war of 1939–45. Unlike its successor, its overall message is 'Comfort ye'. After the violent noise of the Fourth Symphony the listener is struck by the moving, inspiriting gentleness and calm of the Fifth. In the eight years or so that intervened between the two works, the geopolitical state of the world and Vaughan Williams's personal situation had changed dramatically. In the aftermath of the Fourth Symphony he turned again to opera. Here again there was frustration. The light opera *The Poisoned Kiss*, on which he had worked for a number of years, was staged at the Cambridge Arts Theatre in May 1936 and later that year at Sadler's Wells. But this 'Romantic Extravaganza' did not prove to be a success. Opera was not the genre in which Vaughan Williams's great achievements as a composer were to be made. Nevertheless he refused to give up on *The Poisoned Kiss* and tinkered with it until later in his life. In 1937 came the premiere of another opera, a setting of J.M. Synge's powerful, poetic play *Riders to the Sea*. It was performed at the Royal College of Music but was taken no further. This was unfortunate because this musical exploration of human suffering and the stoicism that it elicits constitutes by far the greatest of Vaughan Williams's several attempts at operatic form. Paired with another one-act piece, preferably a comedy, it would be a distinct enrichment of the English opera repertoire.

At the time of these, and many other disappointments and frustrations in the later 1930s, Vaughan Williams came to believe that his creative powers were exhausted. In letters at the time he declared that he would never compose again. He was not to know that more than half of his nine symphonies lay ahead of him.

Some six months after the first run through of *Riders to the Sea* at the Royal College, Vaughan Williams, now sixty-five years old, met Ursula Wood. She was a poet, the wife of an army officer, and had just celebrated her twenty-seventh birthday. She and the composer quickly became lovers and Vaughan Williams's life was transformed.[76] Within eighteen months of the affair beginning the whole of the western world was transformed too, by the outbreak of the Second World War in September 1939. During the early years, which saw a series of military defeats and the London Blitz that took the life of a close young friend, Vaughan Williams worked away at his Fifth Symphony, importing into it material that he had originally intended for another much reworked opera, *The Pilgrim's Progress*.

At one stage in the composition he placed a quotation from Bunyan at the head of the slow movement. It read 'Upon this place stood a cross, and a little sepulchre. Then he said "he hath given me rest by his sorrow, and life by his death".' The words offer a means of coming to terms with the country's many losses at the time. Perhaps Ursula's reassuring presence may also be heard in the renewal and resurrection that are intimated musically in the symphony. He dedicated the work to the contemporary symphonist he most admired: 'Without permission and with the sincerest flattery to Jean Sibelius, whose great example is worthy of imitation.'

The Fifth Symphony had its first orchestral play-through at the BBC's Maida Vale studios on 25 May 1943 with Adrian Boult conducting. The fifteen guests Vaughan Williams invited to this occasion included the members of the music world at the time to whom he was closest: Gerald Finzi, Herbert Howells, Muir Mathieson and Gordon Jacob, his frequent assistant with orchestration. The first public performance took place at a Promenade concert in the Royal Albert Hall on 24 June 1943. By then there was a feeling in the country that at long, long last the course of the war was turning in favour of the Allies. One can hear relief and quiet hope in the music. Since Sir Henry Wood, the founder and presiding figure of the Proms, was ill, Vaughan Williams took his place as conductor. He was pleased with the occasion, reporting to Sir Henry, 'The orchestra were splendid – and as I made no serious mistakes we had a very fine performance.'[77]

It was a great success with those who heard it that summer night. It clearly spoke with insinuating power to an audience bereaved, damaged and wearied by the ongoing war. The first movement, Preludio, begins with horn calls in D major, the ominous, ghostly sound of which must surely have brought to mind the air-raid sirens of very recent experience for those first listeners in a bomb-cratered London. Then comes reassurance, a quietly lyrical theme expressing sympathy, regret, gentle consolation. Meditation follows. A throb of feeling enters and, gathering in intensity, builds to a grand inspiriting swoop of sound. And then a great crescendo. After all the guardedness and reservation in the meditative music, the crescendo releases and sounds out what is fine and indeed noble in life. It is Vaughan Williams's version of what is alluded to in the first theme of Elgar's First Symphony. There follows a modest triumphing and then the music quietens again into reflection. It fades away and there is a return of the disturbing horns. The ending of the first movement is a reminder of the blitzed London under bomb smoke evoked in T.S. Eliot's exactly contemporaneous poem 'Little Gidding', in which a ghostly visitor and mentor, in the manner of Hamlet's father, 'faded on the blowing of the horn'.

The second movement, the Scherzo, is the shortest. It offers a suggestion of high spirits, but enduringly in the background there is melancholy. In the theme for oboe and cor anglais there is also malice: some listeners have been reminded of John Bunyan's 'hobgoblin, nor foul fiend'. There is a chirpy woodwind sound but it does not last long. Cheeriness in this movement is ambiguous, brief and perfunctory. It cannot be maintained and developed. It is suddenly cut off. The third movement, the longest of the four, returns to the dominant mood of the symphony. It is a Romanza that begins with a lament from the solo cor anglais. There follows a sad meditation that is taken over redemptively by a swelling music that moves along in slow, stately fashion. It climaxes in a sweep of rapturous sound that compensates for all the darkness and uncertainty that has gone before. Much of the music in this movement is from the proposed and much reworked opera about Bunyan's pilgrim. It is music of compassion, redemption and reassurance. The Romanza is essentially a reworking of the first movement with the delicately qualified and understated positives given more prominence, extent and power.

The fourth and final movement, the Passacaglia, opens slowly then quickens to a near bouncy beat. A triumphant pealing of bells is suggested. We have moved on to, in more than one sense of the word, celebration. The essentially religious procedure informing the design of this symphony is made clear as the last few minutes take on the character of a benediction and then a recessional. Nevertheless menace remains and cannot be ignored. The symphony concludes with the unnerving horn sounds with which it began. Adrian Boult, hearing the premiere of the symphony on the radio, immediately wrote to Vaughan Williams to congratulate him and to try to express what the symphony meant to him at that moment in the war. He concluded that 'its serene loveliness is completely satisfying in these times and shows, as only music can, what we must work for when this madness is over'.[78] Ursula, a member of the audience at that first performance, remembered how, 'in this radiant performance, fears and despair were cancelled, beauty and serenity were all'. She added, recognizing the devotional aspect of the symphony, that 'the music seemed to many people to bring the peace and blessing for which they longed'.[79]

Vaughan Williams's first five symphonies were written over a period of some thirty-three years. The remaining four took less than a third of that, just some ten years. In his seventies and eighties he resorted urgently to the symphony in order to probe and explore the new sense of humanity, and especially inhumanity, that was one of the concerning legacies of the Second World War. His Sixth Symphony, first performed in 1948, shared its period of gestation with George Orwell's *Nineteen Eighty-Four* and Francis Bacon's *Three Studies for Figures at the Base of a Crucifixion*. It is a profound work that ponders the chaos, destruction and suffering brought about by the Hitler war. It is entirely appropriate that on the morning of the premiere of the Sixth Symphony Vaughan Williams and Ursula should have gone to the retrospective exhibition of the surrealist painter Paul Nash, whose *Totes Meer* (Dead Sea) remains one of the most memorable British paintings of that war.

The Sixth Symphony is a testimony to Vaughan Williams's resilience as a composer, showing how in his seventies he was capable of framing a carefully formulated response to the many horrific shocks brought about by the war years. Richard Capell, a music critic who had admired Vaughan Williams's work for going on forty years, wrote in the *Daily Telegraph*:

Only the great superior artists have so tirelessly renewed the adventure of the spirit.... The Sixth Symphony in E takes a new direction. It will challenge every hearer. The adventurous energy is terrific; and whatever words may be resorted to as a clue, the sheer musical means are compelling and engrossing.... The music says that the soul of man can endure pain and face the troughs of a remoteness beyond the outermost of the planets.[80]

Critics of a younger generation also recognized the intense intellectual ambition and the creative achievement of the work. Desmond Shawe-Taylor was some forty years younger than the composer and a strong advocate of the music of Benjamin Britten, who had long disparaged the music of Vaughan Williams. Writing in the *New Statesman*, Shawe-Taylor observed that the Sixth Symphony represented:

An extraordinary and unpredictable burst of creative activity for a man of 75, in which he seems to have effected a kind of synthesis of the two preceding symphonies, indeed to have summed up the whole of his lifework, but at the same time to have directed a serene and courageous glance into the future, to have meditated on first and last things with a grasp and profundity worthy of Beethoven.[81]

The Sixth Symphony was also enthusiastically received in the United States. When it had its first performance there at the New York Symphony Society, less than a year after its London premiere, the eminent conductor Leopold Stokowski wrote in a programme note, 'This is music that will take its place with the greatest creations of the masters.' And Olin Downes, the music critic of the *New York Times*, also saw the achievement represented by the symphony as 'historic': 'This is one of the most powerful and deeply felt symphonic writings to have appeared since the turn of the century. The sincerity of the expression blazes in every page.'[82]

Accompanying this chorus of admiration were repeated questions and suggestions about what the symphony meant. This happened far more with the Sixth Symphony than any of his other symphonies. Explanations to do with biography and social and political history, it must be repeated, can never be precise. The symphony means what it sounds. And sounds mean beyond and other than what words mean. Michael Kennedy has offered a succinct definition of the meaning of the Sixth Symphony in strictly musical terms: 'First of all it means a closely and logically pursued musical argument on the conflict of major and minor thirds, and the interval of the augmented fourth which sets off more conflicts in keys separated by that interval.'[83]

Nevertheless, as Kennedy goes on to say, Vaughan Williams himself allowed that there was a programmatic, verbally expressible aspect to the work. He referred to Prospero's speech on the transience of human beings at the end of *The Tempest*. And certainly there is a progress in the symphony from the various forms of noisiness in human life to the fading into silence that awaits everyone. Right from the opening bars, full of thunder and violence, like the opening of Shakespeare's play, the listener is involved with powerful emotions and strongly felt experience. There follows over the four movements, if not a narrative then certainly a collocating of aural experiences and developing attempts to reach conclusions from them.

The symphony begins in tumult. Peter Maxwell Davies once commented: 'The extraordinary polyrhythms at the beginning of the Sixth Symphony; they're as advanced as anything in the *Rite of Spring*. They get into your physical system like very little music that I've conducted.'[84] After the violence the music then steadies into a swinging melody. It brings to mind the jazz that was one of the great innovations of the twentieth century and that became increasingly prevalent in British life when a vast American army came over to prepare for the D-Day invasion of continental Europe. With a touch of nostalgia the idiom of English folk music is briefly recalled, but the charming memory of such pastoral is soon swept away, never to return. Other sound worlds have to be confronted. The movement returns to the turmoil of the opening, which was the most enduring, determining sound in Vaughan Williams's symphonies of the 1940s. This starting Allegro concludes with a dull rumble that is disturbing, ominous.

The second movement, Moderato, quickly recalls one of the most famous precipitates of the Second World War, the aggression motif in Shostakovich's *Seventh Symphony*, inspired in great part by the epic siege of Leningrad. A relentlessly repeated, bellicose phrase lasts for some time before giving way to heart-rending moments of wistfulness and hopelessness. These, we will later realize, are a prefiguring of the reflections in the famously subdued, slow and protracted fourth movement Epilogue to this symphony. But now the discordances recur. Advance strongly. Then retreat a little. Reason, compassion, humanity are hung on to by a thread, by a tremulous solo from the cor anglais. But it grows weaker and fades into the background of distant, thudding explosions.

And then the third movement, the Scherzo, crashes in. Its high spirits are ambiguous. The music is cheery but sardonic, spirited but also near demented. The merry, popular ditty of the trio transforms itself into a heavy goose-stepping march. Hitler's *Wehrmacht* is upon us. The sounds of the Second World War weave through this symphony. Also, as Byron Adams has pointed out, 'the saxophone theme sounds suspiciously like a grotesque jazz improvisation on Stephen Foster's "Swanee River", which, under the title "Old Folks At Home", Vaughan Williams had earlier arranged for male chorus ... The overall effect ... is to heighten the jazzy and diabolical aspects of this passage.'[85]

There are also suggestions of the blues, all of them sounds of recent times. But even at its most humane, this double-edged music is no salvation from the cataclysmic shock that has been felt earlier in the work. It comes over as more of an amplification.

Then after the blazing Allegro vivace comes an arresting contrast, the long slow, quiet Epilogue. This was the movement that more than any other in all of Vaughan Williams's nine symphonies provoked among its first and later listeners a search for meaning. Various programmatic allusions have been ascribed to it. It has been suggested, for instance, that this movement evokes a world of post-atomic devastation. Very audibly it is music of sombre meditation. Quietly it wanders, muses, sometimes quickens slightly, sometimes keens. At times it sounds of quiet desperation as it turns and turns about, obsessively seeking progression. Vaughan Williams is unlikely to have known Jean-Paul Sartre's *Huis Clos*, although the 1946 London production, under the title *Vicious Circle*, was broadcast by the BBC. The tormented threshing about in this music, however, is at times affected by the desperate psychological claustrophobia to be found in that play, another product of the war, first produced in Paris in 1944, some four years before the symphony.

Slow clock chimes announce that time is being called on this lengthy, difficult meditation. The music becomes ghostly and runs out into silence. Then comes the surprising aftermath to the symphony; the listener is left not depressed but simply wondering.

Wilfrid Mellers, whose book about Vaughan Williams gives a thorough, strenuously musicological account of the composer's career, found it appropriate to describe this final movement programmatically:

New Street around
the time that Elgar
was a commuter to
Birmingham.

William Stockley, in whose
orchestra Elgar played for
some seven years.

Birmingham Town Hall.

Birmingham University, the building opened by King Edward VII in 1909;
this was the year in which its architect, Aston Webb, also completed the
Victoria and Albert Museum and Admiralty Arch.

Elgar and his wife Alice.

Alice Stuart Wortley.

The Aston Webb Campanile, alluded to by Professor Elgar in his lectures at Birmingham University.

Leith Hill Place in Surrey, where Vaughan Williams spent his childhood.

Vaughan Williams in 1910, at the time of the premiere of the Sea Symphony.

Vaughan Williams haymaking with his wife Adeline. This was the period of his Fourth Symphony.

Vaughan Williams with Adrian Boult on the occasion of the award of the Order of Merit.

MRS GORDON CLARK

Vaughan Williams with E.M. Forster when the composer and writer collaborated on the pageant 'England's Pleasant Land' for the Dorking and Leith Hill Preservation Society.

PHOTOPRESS

Vaughan Williams and his second wife Ursula in the USA in autumn 1954, when he was beginning to contemplate his Eighth Symphony, the brightest of his nine.

VWCT

Benjamin Britten and Peter Pears at The Old Mill, Snape, shortly after their wartime return from the United States.

BRITTEN-PEARS FOUNDATION

Britten, Kathleen Ferrier, Ernest Ansermet and others involved in the first production of 'The Rape of Lucretia' in 1947.

BRITTEN-PEARS FOUNDATION

Benjamin Britten and Rostropovich, June 1976.

NIGEL LUCKHURST/
BRITTEN-PEARS FOUNDATION

Benjamin Britten backstage at the Snape Maltings Concert Hall with Mstislav Rostropovich and Galina Vishnevskaya, 18 June 1976. This was the occasion of the last meeting of the composer and cellist.

NIGEL LUCKHURST/
BRITTEN-PEARS FOUNDATION

Britten, Pears and Imogen Holst in The Red House garden.

ROSAMUND STRODE/
BRITTEN-PEARS FOUNDATION

SCHOSTAKOVITCH

Москва 5 октября 1960 года.

Дорогой

Бенжамин Бриттен!

Спасибо Вам за Вашу телеграмму. Извините, что с таким опозданием отвечаю Вам, так как в поездке я был очень занят.

Примите мои лучшие пожелания.

Горячий почитатель Вашей музыки

/Д. Шостакович/

Moscow, 5th October 1960.
Dear Benjamin Britten,

Thank you for your telegram. Forgive me for replying with such a delay but I was travelling and was very busy.

Please accept my best wishes. Ardent admirer of your music
D. SCHOSTAKOVITCH

Telegram expressing the admiration of Shostakovich for Britten's music, 1960.

BRITTEN-PEARS FOUNDATION

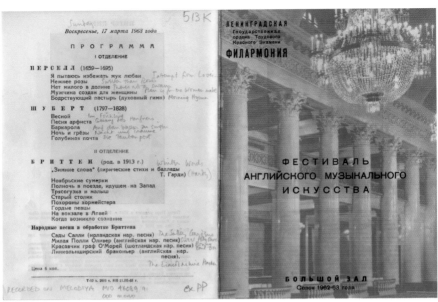

Programme cover and content for a concert in Leningrad (now St Petersburg), 17 March 1963.

the epilogue is perhaps the ultimate auralisation of agnosticism, telling us that The Unknown Region which the hopeful young Vaughan Williams had set out to explore, is not a metaphysical 'other world', but is unknown, and always will be, simply because it is unknowable. The epilogue discovers that in the unknown region there must be nowhere: a fact offering occasion for neither hope nor regret. The difficult faith of the Fifth Symphony is relinquished; man is alone, in the dark, cold and empty desolation. Acceptance brings to this strange music a serene insecurity; a courageous testament of our frightful century.[86]

Certainly this great, extremely subtle work of music can be seen as an attempt, very soon after the events, to render, however obliquely, the unique reverberations of the war that produced the Holocaust and Hiroshima, and to assimilate and come to a conclusion about them. Yet like all great works of art it transcends the specifics of its time. Vaughan Williams himself pointed, as Mellers himself reminds us, to Prospero's summation of the circumscription and transience of human lives.

> We are such stuff
> As dreams are made on, and our little life
> Is rounded with a sleep.

Such philosophical implications in the music, however, are given power and validity by the way it also evokes, through sound, actual specific and very felt experiences. Simon Heffer has noted, for instance, 'the way the jazz saxophone in the scherzo is first brutalised and then snuffed out' as suggesting 'something more than just a Shakespearean vision'. It suggests the short way the Nazis had with jazz, one of the forms they considered to be *entartete Musik* (deformed music). Heffer also recalls the account of one of the origins of the symphony given by Sir Malcolm Sargent, a regular and devoted conductor of the work. Sir Malcolm, presumably as a result of conversations with the composer, pointed to the occasion in March 1941 when a bomb fell on the Café de Paris in the West End of London, killing more than thirty people including the bandleader Ken 'Snakehips' Johnson and members of his West Indian Orchestra. This horrific, barbaric attack on the making of music is one of a number of particular memories evoked by the symphony. The passage in the Scherzo is not the only one. The symphony as a whole seeks tentatively, and without any resounding confident conclusion, to move beyond and above them.

The Sixth Symphony relates a characteristic late Romantic and post-Romantic story, a journey into uncertainty or, put more positively, into what John Keats in a completely different time and generation phrased as 'negative capability'. This occurs, he famously went on to say to his brothers, 'when a man is capable of being in uncertainties, mysteries, doubts, without any irritable reaching after fact and reason'. This is the very psychological and philosophical attitude to be found in the mysterious ending of this carefully worked musical response to the war of 1939–45. The rich and deep complexity of certain passages in Vaughan Williams's art needs to be better recognized. Here, in the concluding, yet inconclusive movement of the tormented Sixth Symphony, is one of the finest examples.

〜

Six months after the first performance of the Sixth Symphony, *Scott of the Antarctic* was chosen for the 1948 Royal Film Performance at the Empire Theatre in Leicester Square. The music accompanying this ambitious production by Ealing Studios was by Vaughan Williams. He had begun writing music for film early in the 1940s as one of his many endeavours to contribute to the patriotic movement known as the War Effort. The music to accompany *Scott of the Antarctic* is the longest and most considerable of the film scores he composed.

This film about Captain Scott's heroic but ultimately doomed attempt to be the first explorer to reach the South Pole belongs with many expressions of national pride that followed the victory achieved in 1945. Throughout the country there was a mood of self-congratulation and triumphalism. The Ealing Studios film director Charles Frend was responsible for the extremely successful *The Cruel Sea*, which is a salute to the endurance and heroism of Navy personnel who fought the costly war against the U-boats in the North Atlantic. Frend also directed *Scott of the Antarctic*, but this film transcends a simple stimulation of patriotic feeling. It is an insightful examination of the character of the hero and an affecting account of the tragic end that befell him. Vaughan Williams's music matches the film in poetry and resonance. It is illuminating that we now have a published recording of the complete score, transcribed and conducted by Martin Yates, including the passages that were not used in the finished film. It shows very clearly why the composer should decide that this sequence of musical passages had the making of a symphony, the one that would become his seventh. The recording also reveals how fundamentally different these programmatic pieces are from the symphonic structure and semantic system that he later made out of them. In a letter to Alan Frank, his editor at Oxford University Press, Vaughan Williams toyed with the idea of not mentioning 'the connection with the Scott film'[87] in the naming of the symphony. He clearly saw it as a composition that could stand independently.

In the same letter, with characteristic modesty he spoke of the work as 'a mere bit of carpentry'. But it is audibly far, far more than this. It is a symphony of great power and thematic intricacy. With the title Sinfonia (an Italian term recalling Corelli) pointing us to an early stage in the history of symphonic form, the *Sinfonia Antartica* gives us a world far vaster than any baroque interior and the music that might be heard there. But it continues the dialectical method inherent in symphonic form as a way of bringing order into what is experienced and expressed. And what an overwhelming experience the symphony reports and contemplates! Ambitiously it ponders, in generally sombre tones, the dualism that is the relationship of human consciousness to the incalculable vastness of the cosmos that surrounds it.

Starting with the words of its title, *Sinfonia Antartica*, the seventh symphony proved to be the most explicitly programmatic of the Vaughan Williams nine. Each of the five movements has a literary quotation for its epigraph (in some early performances of the symphony these were spoken by an actor). The music thus has direct, immediate references to extra-musical entities. The first quotation, from Shelley, defining and saluting the human capacity to endure and prevail against the very worst trials, is the verbal confirmation of the heavy, dogged persistence that is sounded in the opening music of the first movement. It is a perseverance that must withstand the unnerving wailing of choir, soprano and orchestra conveying the great inhuman wastes of this planet and of the universe beyond. The use of the wind machine enhances the desolation in the movement.

The one moment of light relief in the symphony comes with the second movement, the Scherzo. For the superscription Vaughan Williams quotes Psalm 104:26: 'There go the ships and there is that Leviathan'. The disjunction between the whale, the great creature at home in the deep, and the frail human constructs devised to sail on it is developed with some humour in the course of the movement. Other sea creatures are here as well. A perky tune for trombone and trumpet mimics the waddle of penguins. There are other seabirds, too, the orchestral onomatopoeias suggesting their sounds, cries and movements. But there are also occasional disturbing interruptions; these are ominous sounds that bring to mind the danger, the vulnerability, the precariousness of those setting out on unknown seas.

After the marine creatures move off and away into silence there comes the third and longest of the five movements. It is entitled 'Landscape' and this refers to an art form other than music or poetry. The literary reference is to Coleridge's rapt awe at the prospect of the creation of the glaciers in his poem 'Hymn before Sunrise, in the Vale of Chamouni'. A poem with a title invoking music, its last five words might be the title of a 'terrific' painting by Turner. The movement is a powerful evocation of a vast terrain, utterly inhospitable to human beings. The music now sounds very much of the twentieth century, even modernist. It is far, far removed from what was heard in the two symphonies from before the First World War. Aided by organ and again by wind machine, the orchestra conveys disturbingly the grinding of ice upon ice, its cracking and melting into the waters. The block chords confirm the high drama of these processes so much vaster than those of human beings. Horns and flutes suggest the uncompromising, frozen immobility of the Antarctic background. There comes a lashing, cutting wind that finally abates only to leave the listener with a sense of emptiness, nothingness similar to that explored in the final movement of the Sixth Symphony.

But this psychological and geographical landscape is by no means the last word in the *Sinfonia Antartica*. In the next movement, the Intermezzo, a lyrical piping from the oboe brightly reminds us of the powers of persistence of the human spirit. Vaughan Williams in the epigraph to the movement refers to two lines from a lyric poem by John Donne asserting the endurance of human love. As it moves towards its conclusion this section of the symphony allows hints of a funeral march, but the ending, although elegiac in mood, reiterates and commemorates in delicate harp chords this essential and irreducible fact of experience.

The fifth and final movement, the Epilogue, is a move to resolving the dialectic that runs through the symphony. The desolating blasts, the cutting winds and tempest are back again. But there is also a music of briskness and of the stoical common sense that echoes the spirit of the words from Captain Scott's diary that head the movement. The opening brings sounds of busy, purposeful activity. Then comes determined marching. But this is lost in the sounds of immeasurably larger forces, the ferocious sounds of Antarctic weather. The composer – we sense his voice – ends the symphony with a compassionate, quiet, resigned lament as orchestral music fades and we are left with the inhuman wind machine conveying the sounds of a gale and blown snow. The final bars also invite us perhaps to remember the ending of the previous symphony and also that of the third symphony, the *Pastoral*. The later symphonies, on several occasions, make reference to their predecessors and in this way intimate that there is among the nine symphonies a larger and connected musical narrative.

The symphony had its first performance in Manchester on 14 January 1953. It was played by the Hallé Orchestra conducted by Sir John Barbirolli, very much an enthusiast for the music of Vaughan Williams. After the final movement faded away into silence, there was, understandably, a protracted silence. But once the applause started it went on and on. Vaughan Williams left his seat to join Barbirolli on the stage and the applause surged wildly, the audience rising to its feet. *The Sinfonia Antartica* enjoyed a less puzzled, more unambiguously successful reception than its predecessor.

This was even more the case with his next. The entirely different Eighth Symphony appeared little over two years later. It was first performed on 2 May 1956 by the same orchestra and conductor in the same venue. Vaughan Williams was now eighty-two years of age. He had yet another symphony to compose.

The first performance of the Eighth Symphony was even more of a triumph than that of the *Sinfonia Antartica*. When the jokey second movement, the *Scherzo alla Marcia*, was played laughter rang out in the Free Trade Hall. At the end of the concert Ursula and the composer were surrounded and pursued by reporters as they tried to make their way back to their hotel. Twelve days later when the symphony was heard for the first time in London, at the Royal Festival Hall, the reception was again rapturous. Vaughan Williams appeared on the stage beside Sir John Barbirolli and the entire audience rose to applaud and cheer. The success of the Eighth Symphony spread rapidly and the work was played at venues throughout Europe. It clearly spoke to the times. In New York in October 1956, in the approach to the Suez crisis, Eugene Ormandy and the Philadelphia Orchestra gave the first American performance. Ormandy wrote warmly to Vaughan Williams to tell him of its enthusiastic reception: 'every performance was greeted with shouts of bravo and prolonged applause, something we rarely hear after a first performance of a new work these days.'[88]

The New York Critics' Circle voted it the best symphonic work of 1956.

One simple factor in Vaughan Williams's achievement as Britain's greatest symphonist was his longevity. He produced at least one symphony in and of each of the first six decades of the twentieth century. The result was a large-scale musical representation of each of the strikingly different decades in the life of the nation and in his own eventful life. It was appropriate that when in the 1950s he entered his eighties he should be recognized by the leading young dramatist of the day as the musical spokesman for his time. The play *Look Back in Anger* by the twenty-seven-year-old John Osborne had its first night at the Royal Court Theatre in the very same week that Vaughan Williams's Eighth Symphony was premiered by Sir John Barbirolli in Manchester. We remember the play as one of the most distinctive and characteristic texts of the 1950s. In it the hero, the relentlessly sneering social iconoclast Jimmy Porter, cites and invokes Vaughan Williams as the voice of late imperial England, which he triumphantly, yet also regretfully, declares to be disappearing.

Jimmy Porter cannot have been aware of the supranational concerns that dominate Vaughan Williams's symphonies, or of the philosophical questions they address. In their metaphysical concerns they are very different from the *English Folk Song Suite* for military band and the many similar compositions that Jimmy Porter might well have had in mind. Nevertheless in Vaughan Williams's Eighth Symphony, almost exactly contemporaneous with Osborne's play, a pastoral world of woodnotes wild, so often associated with Vaughan Williams's name, is in fact evoked in the opening bars. But as always what follows must have surprised its first listeners. Each of the composer's symphonies stands in marked, dramatic contrast to its predecessor.

The Eighth is a rare item in symphonic literature, a symphony about happiness and contentment. In Vaughan Williams's case these were hard won. After the upset that attended the death of his first wife Adeline and the ending of a marriage that had lasted well over half a century, Vaughan Williams gave up his suburban home in Surrey. These upheavals were made more pointed by complications attaching to his relationship with Ursula. The pain of this particular situation is, as I have pointed out in my biography of the composer, to be heard most vividly in his Violin Sonata in A minor, first performed in 1954.[89] But by the time he was completing the Eighth Symphony Vaughan Williams was a settled man. He and Ursula were now man and wife and living in a grand house in a Nash terrace on the north-western edge of Regent's Park. It was a time of great happiness for both of them. Ursula was to characterize those years in the title of her memoirs: *Paradise Remembered*. This was the context of the new symphony.

The Eighth stands in pointed contrast to its two most immediate predecessors, which address, for the most part sombrely, the bleakness of experience. The brightest and shortest of the nine symphonies, the Eighth charms from the outset. Humorously, the first movement, Fantasia, is subtitled 'Variazioni senza tema' or, perhaps we may infer, variations in search of a theme. Is Elgar being remembered? The symphony begins lightly with a lilting, piping melody and later in the Fantasia this pleasing, gently flowing lyricism will recur. But the movement is more than merely charming. There is conspicuously intricate thematic development. On occasion there comes a scurrying, raucous percussion and an urgent building up to heavy dramatic insistence. The music of this composer, we are reminded, is not unaware of violent conflicts in life. But here in the symphony the overall context makes it sound like a filtered memory, a passing reminder. At the end of the movement we are brought back to the gentle piping as the music trails slowly and quietly away.

The Scherzo, which so amused that first audience in Manchester, is a perky piece and unfailingly cheerful. The composer is determined to entertain; he concludes this second movement with a jolly pastoral dance and a twiddle of a finish. The third movement, the Cavatina, played entirely by the string sections of the orchestra, requires the audience to be a little more serious. A part of the overall charm strategy directing the symphony is an invitation to savour the pleasures of instrumentation. The bouncy rhythms of the preceding Scherzo, performed by wind instruments alone, are now replaced by long, flowing Elgarian lines with the violins leading the rest of the strings. We are taken back briefly to the gentle melancholy to be found in many of Vaughan Williams's earlier works. The opening lyrical melody has a touch of sadness that becomes increasingly palpable and textured as the strings pulse ever more strongly. Then the emotion abates as a solo violin reminds us, in a subdued fashion, of the ascending lark of yesteryear – and indeed of its reappearance in the much more recent Violin Sonata. After such autobiographical references the Cavatina ends mooningly and in the closing bars becomes serene.

But at the beginning of the last movement, Toccata, the composer sounds the gong resoundingly, echoing the gong that used to be the summons to mealtimes in stately homes and seaside boarding houses. But here we are summoned instead to a feast of instruments and instrumentation. In his note to the symphony Vaughan Williams remarked that the opening is a 'rather sinister exordium'. And though this phrase might lead us to wonder what subversives might be present at the party, it does not spoil our fiesta. All is now joyous and celebratory. The music moves along merrily, the bells ring out climactically and we end with a grand emphatic finale. This is the only one of Vaughan Williams's nine symphonies to end loudly. Hospitably the composer bids us farewell with the gift of a profound gaiety such as W.B. Yeats, himself approaching the end of his comparably long career as a poet, imagined in his poem 'Lapis Lazuli'. The stone shows figures of musicians from ancient China whose

> Accomplished fingers begin to play.
> Their eyes mid many wrinkles, their eyes,
> Their ancient, glittering eyes, are gay.

But gaiety was not to be the mood in which Vaughan Williams's long lifetime of symphonies concluded. Less than two years after the first joyous performance of the Eighth he produced one more symphony. It had its premiere on 12 April 1958, performed by the Royal Philharmonic Orchestra with Sir Malcolm Sargent conducting. None of the other symphonies were so close to each other in terms of first performances as these last two: and they are very much complementary works, the sombre fatedness dominating the Ninth offering a stern proviso to the good spirits of the Eighth. It is a major work emanating from the introspections of old age.

The critical reception of the Ninth Symphony in 1958 was by no means as warm as that which had greeted its lighter, brighter predecessor. In a year that saw the premieres of new works by much younger composers such as Peter Maxwell Davies, Thea Musgrave and Cornelius Cardew, music critics failed to see anything new or of interest in Vaughan Williams's last symphony. One reviewer spoke of 'composing for the sake of composing'. Another declared that the themes 'plainly resemble the themes of his other works'. The second movement was said to be 'silly', even 'asinine'. Painfully disappointed, Vaughan Williams felt that he had outlived his time. The morning after the first performance, a friend (presumably Michael Kennedy) asked the composer what he thought of these unsympathetic notices. The eighty-five-year old replied, 'I don't think they can quite forgive me for still being able to do it at my age'.[90]

Unfortunately Vaughan Williams was not to live to see the appreciation and understanding that commentators have shown in more recent years. The Ninth Symphony is manifestly a work of great thematic richness that shows a delicate, subtle probing of both music and experience. As with the previous symphonies, it is infused with literary references. Vaughan Williams once connected the ending of *A London Symphony* with the concluding paragraphs of *Tono-Bungay* by H.G. Wells. More than forty years later his final symphony is very much informed by the stoical, compassionate pessimism expressed in the concluding lines of Thomas Hardy's *Tess of the D'Urbervilles* as the author contemplates and comments on Tess as a tragic figure thrown about like a plaything by the President of the Immortals. Vaughan Williams had admired this novel intensely throughout his life and, as Alain Frogley demonstrates in his illuminating study of the work, it was very much in his mind (and actually alluded to in his sketches) as he composed his final symphony.[91]

A stoical, Hardyesque melancholy pervades the work right from the doleful chords with which the work begins. A bright, cheering lyrical theme intrudes on this heavy insistence but, as later in the movement, is swiftly swept away by the pounding, fateful forces. And then we are in a world of eerie desolation with the flugelhorn darkly pondering. In his very detailed reading of the symphony Wilfrid Mellers wonders, interestingly, whether Vaughan Williams 'might have taken a hint from Miles Davis's haunting use of the flugelhorn in his recordings during the fifties'.[92] Vaughan Williams's version of the blues builds to a sequence of unhappy climaxes before the music falls mournfully into silence. The second movement, the Andante sostenuto, asserts a theme that expresses nobility, but this is soon interrupted by a barbaric beat that Vaughan Williams associated with the ghostly drummer of Salisbury Plain who figured in R.H. Barham's *Ingoldsby Legends*. As he composed, the Tess country, which he knew so well and walked so often, was very much in his thoughts. The barbaric rhythms are repeated; they become ever more sinister and threatening. Then comes an attempt to evade them, a completely different rhythm, a swaying, dancing passage, another attempt at happier movement. But then the ominous sounds return more heavily and crushingly than before. More is heard of the earlier lyrical melancholy that now moons along, lost and forlorn, before as at the end of the first movement it fades to a silent conclusion.

The jokiness of the third movement, the Scherzo, seems coarsely irrelevant The crude beat of the marching band and music hall routines jig away in the background without obscuring the ongoing, haunted refrain that is made up of the sounds of human vulnerability. There is in it a painful feeling of solitariness and isolation. The chorale theme played by the saxophone hints touchingly at the possibility of redemption. But this is not pursued in the final movement. The controlling mood here is wistful, persistently elegiac throughout the highly complex contrapuntal interweaving. Melancholy lingers, wanders, turns about showing changing colours. But then the large decisive forces intervene. Hardyesque and fateful, they force themselves in and settle matters. Their power builds and heightens. And then come the great hammer blows that speak of mortality and the destined, unavoidable conclusion of human life. We are reminded of similar dramatic intrusions at the end of Mahler's Sixth Symphony and the Fifth Symphony of Sibelius. Three concluding and conclusive blows: first one, then a second and then the third, all of them destructive and decisive. All that is left after the mighty, apocalyptic blows are the fading harp glissandi that are the rippling of their aftermath.

〜

And so ended Vaughan Williams's near half-century career as a symphonist. A battered stoicism shields and contains the lyrical notes of tenderness and hope. The work on this last symphony took less than a year. He first mentioned a 'flirtation' with a new symphony in August 1957 and it had its first performance in the first week of April 1958. It was the most rapidly composed of all nine. During these months he was fiercely protective and jealous of his time. Declining an invitation from an acquaintance of nearly fifty years, he wrote, 'I fear I ought not to do it – October and early November are always great productive times with me … So I must keep the rest of the time free for my work.'[93] Within months of his death he worked strenuously with symphonic form. When the Ninth was finished he was keen that all the working that lay behind it should be made public. He did not want the symphony to be seen as a rushed job. When an exhibition of his manuscripts at the Royal Festival Hall was prepared, he was anxious that all the preliminary drafts for the Ninth should be shown:

> I should like them to show the whole of the scaffolding so to speak, including about 12 rough notebooks and a rough full score, 2 rough copies in some cases … I usually destroy my rough copies, but I have kept these as I thought it might be useful to show the scaffolding.[94]

When, in the middle of writing the Ninth Symphony, he celebrated his eighty-fifth birthday, he received the tribute of a number of works that fellow composers had written for the occasion. Writing to thank one of them, Edmund Rubbra, Vaughan Williams made plain his belief in the dedication and the sense of high calling that music entailed. To the younger composer he wrote of his gift, 'It gives a feeling of continuity to the great art which we serve and will insure that the line goes on unbroken from generation to generation.'[95] Vaughan Williams's Ninth Symphony takes an important place in the line of English symphonies begun by Edward Elgar nearly fifty years before.

3

Benjamin Britten

S IR EDWARD ELGAR, OM, died in February 1934. It was a time when the sixty-one-year-old Vaughan Williams was pondering those several discontents of the period between the wars, the unhappiness and nastiness of which were to thunder out in the music of his Fourth Symphony, which for his admirers was so shockingly different from anything that he had composed before.

In that same month Benjamin Britten, a young man of twenty from Lowestoft, was nervously preparing for the first performance of one of the first compositions of his adulthood. This was A *Boy Was Born*, a sequence of choral pieces concerning Christ's Nativity. The work marked the emergence of what was to prove to be, chronologically speaking, the third great creative talent in English music of the twentieth century. After the death of Vaughan Williams in 1958, Britten was unquestionably the leading figure in British music; and far more so than his two great predecessors, he commanded an audience overseas.

His music, like his social and political attitudes, differed profoundly from those of his predecessors. Towards the work of Vaughan Williams, whom he first encountered as an eminence and as a senior teacher at the Royal College of Music, where Britten was a student, the younger man was unfailingly critical, even disdainful, sometimes even mocking. His dismissal of the music of Elgar was similarly curt. In his journal he deplored 'the exaggerated sentimentality and nobilmenti of Elgar's 1st symphony', adding, 'I swear that only in Imperialist England would such a work be tolerated.'[96]

Britten's intellectual and artistic evolution, as we see it recorded in the vividly descriptive diary he kept from 1928 to 1938 – from just before his fourteenth birthday until some five months before his twenty-fifth – is in one important respect an account of his gradual disassociation from Imperial England. Nevertheless that was the social order into which he was born in November 1913, less than a year before the beginning of that Great War that was to begin a radical transformation of Britain and of its standing in the world. Along with his three siblings he had, as the son of a prosperous dentist in Lowestoft, all the comforts and privileges of a well-to-do middle-class home. At Gresham's School, Holt, he received a public school education and, aside from his intense and exceptional musical interest, shared many of the pastimes of his school contemporaries. He especially enjoyed tennis, both as a reasonably competent player and as a keen follower of Wimbledon.

His diversion from the norms of his class began with his early attraction to pacifism. While a student at the Royal College of Music, and still very much a churchgoer, he would go from his lodgings at 173 Cromwell Road to attend services at St Michael's Church in Chester Square in Belgravia. Here at the age of nineteen he was greatly impressed by an anti-war sermon presented by the vicar, the Reverend W.H. Elliot. It was, the teenage student noted, 'the most incredibly brilliant and moving sermon on War'.[97] This was in 1933, the year in which Hitler came to power in Germany. The following year supporters of the League of Nations, the predecessor of the United Nations, launched an initiative called the Peace Ballot. They distributed nationwide a questionnaire asking five questions to do with the League and the concept of peace through collective security that it sought to promote. The subtext was an offer to the public of an opportunity to show its support for the League and for the exercise of international law in keeping the peace in face of the aggressive regimes now controlling Italy and Germany. A leaflet accompanying and explaining the ballot declared that, in voting for the League of Nations' policies, 'you are helping not only your country, but the other countries of the world to maintain Peace and abolish war with all its horrors.' Britten quickly volunteered his services in support of the initiative and went from door to door in his area of Lowestoft distributing the ballots. He commented that it was 'A foul job – but it may do a little good, and make a few people use their brains.' Unfortunately the neighbourhood was not particularly supportive of the peace cause. He added, 'But of course it would be my luck to get allotted a road just packed with diehards – Indian colonels, army widows, typical old spinsters etc!'[98]

The campaign for peace, inspired in great part by painful memories of the hideous atrocities of the First World War, took other forms. In 1934 Dick Sheppard, a former Dean of Canterbury Cathedral and vicar of St Martin-in-the-Fields, and a military chaplain early in the war, published a letter in the *Manchester Guardian* inviting readers to send him a postcard pledging never to support war: within days he had received 135,000 cards. From this massive and unexpected surge of support originated an organization known as the Peace Pledge Union. Britten was very much supportive and in collaboration with a fellow pacifist, the writer Ronald Duncan, who became a lifelong friend, wrote a rallying song for the movement entitled *Pacifist March*.

As the young man's commitment to the peace cause intensified, so too did his interest in and sympathy with left-wing political attitudes, and more specifically Marxist ones, which were such a prominent feature of British intellectual life in the 1930s. For Britten, one of those moments that can suddenly bring about the redirection of a life and career came with a telephone call on 26 April 1935 from the secretary of Edward Clark, a BBC music producer. He had taken an interest in Britten's student compositions and indeed conducted his Opus One, his *Sinfonietta*, in a broadcast performance. The BBC, Britten learned, had been approached by the General Post Office film unit and asked to recommend someone who might be able to supply a musical score for one of their documentaries. Britten immediately set off to where the GPO film unit had its studios in Blackheath, south-east London. After a lunch with one of the producers, the highly experienced film-maker Alberto Cavalcanti, Britten was employed to write the music to accompany a film about the Jubilee postage stamp, which was to be issued as a part of the celebrations marking the twenty-five years of the reign of King George V. And so, at the age of twenty-one, began Britten's career composing for the film industry, which was to be an important part of his life for the rest of the 1930s. His introduction into the milieu of documentary film-making greatly broadened his education, bringing him into contact with people who were at the cutting edge in the other arts. Far more than either Elgar or Vaughan Williams, Britten was close to practising painters and poets. One of those present at that first interview lunch at Blackheath was the artist William Coldstream, who was known as one of the country's most progressive painters. Some five years older than Britten, Coldstream, like Auden, already had some standing in the arts. Earlier in his career he had produced abstract works such as were unfamiliar to the British public, but he was now in the process of turning to a realistic rendering of ordinary, mundane life. This kind of readily accessible representationalism would be the leading characteristic of the Euston Road School, which he founded in association with Lawrence Gowing, Claude Rogers and Victor Pasmore. This aesthetic was readily compatible with 'the creative treatment of actuality', which was the phrase used by John Grierson, the great documentary film-maker and director of the GPO Film Unit, to encapsulate his aims.

Coldstream directed *The King's Stamp* and was also the editor of the second film that Britten scored for the GPO Film Unit, *Coal Face*, which portrayed the life of a Scottish mining community with all its hardships and dangers. Britten then went on to write the music for *Night Mail*, which has enjoyed the most enduring fame of all the films produced by John Grierson's organization. This is in part due to the verse commentary written by W.H. Auden to accompany, along with Britten's music, the concluding minutes of the film: 'This is the night mail crossing the border, bringing the cheque and the postal order.'

Of all the creative talents that Britten encountered at the Blackheath studios, Wystan Hugh Auden was by far the most powerful influence on him. Over the next few years Auden was to play the leading role in Britten's intellectual, artistic and emotional development. There is evidence too, in poems and letters, that Auden contributed to Britten's coming to terms with his homosexuality.

Six years older than the composer, Auden was an established poet at the time the two first met at the film studios. On the strength of his volume *Poems*, published in 1930, his verse drama *The Dance of Death* (1933) and the play *The Dog Beneath the Skin*, first produced early in 1936 and which he wrote in collaboration with his then lover Christopher Isherwood, Auden was regarded at that time as the leader of the second generation of modernist poets in the English language. The modernist poetic first introduced in and by the collaboration between T.S. Eliot and Ezra Pound in the 1910s was, some twenty years later, inherited and developed by a new generation that was commonly referred to as the Auden Group. Prominent among those who wrote under his commanding literary leadership were Stephen Spender, Christopher Isherwood and Louis MacNeice.

Auden, like William Coldstream, was a considerable intellectual force. When he was first in their company Britten was greatly intimidated by the wide range of their reading and knowledge. In September 1935, for instance,

Britten met up with them at the headquarters of the GPO Film Unit in central London. In his diary he noted. 'Spent day with Coldstream and Auden in Soho Sq. and British Museum etc. ... I always feel very young and stupid when with these brains – I mostly sit silent when they hold forth about subjects in general. What brains!'[99]

Before he met Auden, Britten's mental development had centred on his intense musical education, which was principally directed by his mentor and friend, the composer Frank Bridge. Outside music his reading, after he left school, had been a matter of unsystematic borrowing from the local public library and from that middle-class institution of the day, the Boots Book-lovers' Library. Britten's reading became wider under Auden's influence, far more serious and intellectually ambitious. The Auden poets of the 1930s were greatly interested in the materialist philosophy that was the basis of Marxism and in the dialectical movement, which Marx saw as an inherent feature of matter. An important Marxist theorist in Britain at the time was Rajani Palme Dutt, who was also a prominent member of the Executive Committee of the Communist Party of Great Britain. In 1934, as Hitler acted swiftly to consolidate the Nazi regime in Germany, Palme Dutt published his *Fascism and Social Revolution: A Study of the Economics and Politics of the Extreme Stages of Capitalism in Decay*. Britten read the book as he lazed on a beach in early August 1935. A year later his study of left-wing thought was continuing. As he prepared for another seaside holiday in July 1936, Marx was one of the authors he chose to buy as he went 'rummaging in Charing X Road for books to read in Cornwall'.[100]

As Britten became ever more involved with Auden, his sympathy with communism and with the philosophy of dialectical materialism increased. Even before he became friends with the poet, however, he had been interested in the subject: in the summer of 1935 he wrote in his diary that he had tried 'to talk communism with Mum, but it is impossible to say anything to anyone brought up in the old order without severe ruptions. The trouble is that fundamentally she agrees with me and won't admit it.'[101] Some four months later he was writing a considered letter on politics to a lady of his mother's generation who had founded a local amateur orchestra that Britten occasionally conducted. It was, he noted in his journal, 'a long letter in defence of Communism – not a difficult letter to write! It has shocked a lot of people that I am interested in the subject!'[102] His Marxist views were more than a matter of startling members of his middle-class circle. His proletarian sympathies extended beyond the philosophical. In the same diary entry he recorded that he was 'preparing two Grocery (and Coal and Meat etc.), parcels for poor families here'. His sister Barbara, later to be a hospital matron, helped him choose the items to be given to local people in need.

Britten's commitment to practical action, however, did not extend as far as contemplating going to Spain, as Auden did, at the time of the country's civil war, which for the left throughout the North Atlantic countries presented the most immediate political challenge. Auden's fine and unduly neglected poem 'Spain 1937' shows a keen, highly educated sense of the Marxist notion of the workings of the dialectic and of its clear visibility at certain world-historical moments. For Auden, as for many others, Spain at the time of its civil war revealed just such a historical turning point. The French Revolution of a century and a half before, which marked the ending of the feudal and aristocratic order, was another. This way of reading history would remain with Britten long after he and Auden had lost interest in Marxism. A sense of the pivotal, historical moment is to a greater or lesser extent the basis of Britten's sequence of operatic masterpieces that begin with *Peter Grimes* in 1945. In particular it is the assumption that underlies the verbal and musical intricacy of *Billy Budd*.

Britten will surely have been impressed by 'Spain 1937', by its rhetorical power, its arresting stanzaic collages and the rush of telling imagery with which, cinematographically, Auden evokes long historical vistas. It is an important poem, very representative of its decade. Auden's literary influence on Britten was more important and long lasting than his political leanings. For Britten, as indeed for Auden himself, communism proved to be a passing influence rather than a matter of serious commitment. Neither ever actually joined the Communist Party of Great Britain.

Auden was Britten's inspirational mentor and greatly expanded his literary horizons. He was also his literary collaborator. They completed several works together. *Four Cabaret Songs*, which was one of their lighter works, shows how, presumably through Auden and his friends, Britten learned something of the satiric idiom of the German writer Bertolt Brecht and the texts he produced for Kurt Weill and Hanns Eisler. The poet Rainer Maria Rilke was a stimulus to a more serious piece. The co-translator into English of Rilke's major work *The Duino Elegies* was Auden's close friend Stephen Spender. Rilke's highly distinctive poetry was much discussed in a wide range of artistic groups in the 1930s. It was, for instance, an important mode of feeling and perception for the then emerging sculptor Barbara Hepworth. And it is a prime and subtle influence on the ambitious orchestral song cycle that Auden and Britten wrote together, *Our Hunting Fathers*.

Writing in the *New Republic*, Auden contrasted Rilke with Shakespeare. The latter, he maintained, 'thought of the non-human world in terms of the human'; Rilke, on the other hand, showed, 'the human in terms of the non-human ... A way of thought which ... Is more characteristic of the child than of the adult.'[103] Early on in the first of the *Duino Elegies* the human condition is glimpsed from an animal perspective. The difficult German of one of the lines may be translated as: 'And the clever animals are fully aware that we are not very securely at home in the commonly interpreted world.'[104]

The literary strategy directing *Our Hunting Fathers* is the use of animals to show different aspects and different limitations of human consciousness. The text Auden created is a highly accomplished literary work comprising the selection and collation of three found poems and two original ones by Auden himself; these constitute the introduction and the finale to the sequence. The first poem compared the uncertainties of the 'we' of the present with the questionable confidence of those of an earlier stage in human history, our hunting fathers. The 'we' are incapable of self-definition, patients not agents, morally paralysed and changeable only by an external cataclysmic force:

> We cannot voluntarily move
> but await the extraordinary compulsion of the deluge
> and the earthquake.

This emotional and moral suspendedness, so reminiscent of the passage in Rilke's poetry, is followed by the three middle sections, which are satirical, both verbally and musically. The first, 'Rats Away!', based on an anonymous medieval text 'modernised by W.H. Auden', evokes the unnerving scurry of a plague of rats, then chants the whining, inadequate liturgy that a priestly human voice employs in attempting to exorcize the frightening vermin. The mode of human uncertainty, such as Rilke spoke of, here communicates itself as a shudder that is in no way modified by the laughably unconvincing liturgical response. As Donald Mitchell has observed, after the singer's final Amen, 'the orchestra's brilliant and unbroken scale leaves us in no doubt that it is the rats who have triumphed and not the prayer.' A striking feature of *Our Hunting Fathers*, a very early work by Britten, is the highly effective way in which the words and music complement each other. The final passage of 'Rats Away!' is an excellent instance, introducing, as Mitchell goes on to say,

> through purely musical means, a symbolic and dramatic meaning which the text alone certainly does not offer. The image of humankind swamped by vermin and in peril of defeat – the old nostrums having lost their power – remains a very potent one. It must have seemed especially relevant to the youthful Auden and Britten in the summer of 1936.[105]

'Messalina', the third of the five sections of *Our Hunting Fathers*, mocks the sentimentality of the notoriously lecherous Roman Empress in her doting on a pet monkey. Here is an entirely different relationship with the animal world from that in the preceding song. Messalina may go about 'a-crying', but the music very audibly mocks her 'heigh-hos'. The funereal slowness of the playing in the third and fourth lines pokes fun at the extravagance and incontinence of Messalina's desires. The monkey is clearly not 'her only treasure'. Human beings can be as inordinate in their desire for each other as in their love for animals. As Messalina's 'Fie, Fie, Fies' die unhappily away, Britten ends with a postlude, dominated by the harp and flute, which ironically offers an extended bluesy finish.

The penultimate song in the cycle is entitled 'Dance of Death (Hawking for the Partridge)'. Auden took the text from the work of the Jacobean composer Thomas Ravenscroft. The cycle is as much about our literary fathers as it is about our reactionary ancestors who hunted. There is a hectic violence in the music that accompanies words evoking the occasion of hawking for partridge. Unpleasantly the music conveys human pleasure and complacency in setting creature upon creature. The unobtrusive entry of folk song towards the end points up the antiquity of such an activity, but the work suddenly has a keenly felt contemporary relevance with the insertion of 'German and Jew' into the hunting cries. The bloodlust in the Jacobean text shows itself again in the anti-Semitic horrors of Hitler's recently established regime in Germany.

The work ends as it had begun with words in modern English written by Auden. They are less readily understandable than the passages that come between. They are more self-conscious, more strained, more Rilkean. They make up two stanzas, each of ten lines that have but the faintest suggestion of half-rhyming. The second, the more difficult of the two, is a question. The tortured sentence construction struggles against the lineation as it seeks to conclude whether what our hunting fathers complacently regarded as the lesser consciousness of the animal would have been bettered by some evolutionary addition of what constitutes human consciousness, human being. The doubt and uncertainty in the words are tellingly enhanced by the questioning in the meditative xylophone part with which Britten concludes the work.

Our Hunting Fathers was premiered at the Norwich Festival in September 1936. A rehearsal for the performance had taken place in London a few days earlier. In his diary Britten described the occasion as the 'most catastrophic evening of my life'. The members of the London Philharmonic Orchestra started to snigger at the music that was put before them. The 'Rats' section, he remembered, brought shrieks of laughter and he got 'hot and desperate', getting 'a lot of the speeds wrong and very muddled'.[106] Perhaps even more mortifying for the twenty-two-year old conductor was that the humiliating situation was retrieved by Vaughan Williams, the grey-haired eminence from the Royal College of Music whom Britten in his diary, and doubtless in conversation, had consistently deplored, scorned and mocked. Vaughan Williams it was who now entered the disorderly rehearsal room and commandingly intervened, ordering the orchestra members to treat the young man's music with some respect. Which they immediately did.

Vaughan Williams's *Five Tudor Portraits* had its premiere on the very same programme at the Norwich Festival as *Our Hunting Fathers*. But while Britten's piece elicited mixed reviews and bewildered responses, Vaughan Williams's new work was 'very successful': 'not my music but obviously the music for the audience',[107] Britten conceded. There is a point of comparison between the two works; each contains a lament for the death of a pet animal. Britten's 'Messalina' mocks keenly the sentimentality, the grotesquely disproportionate feelings of the Empress. Vaughan Williams sets 'Jane Scroop (Her Lament for Philip Sparrow)' by the Tudor poet John Skelton, a dramatic monologue spoken by a little girl whose beloved pet sparrow has been killed by a cat. It is music of gentle compassion governing an amused indulgence of the young child's sequence of hyperbolic responses to the death of her pet. The text that Vaughan Williams set is a much longer and more considerable work than that of Britten's 'Messalina' and his music conveys a greater, simpler and more confident humaneness. What alone distinguishes the Britten setting is the stylish irony, especially in the postlude.

After *Our Hunting Fathers* Auden and Britten grew closer to each other.

It is clear that the poet became strongly attracted sexually to the younger man. They also continued their creative collaborations. Under the title *On This Island* Britten made settings of some of the poems, all about various aspects of love, from Auden's *Look, Stranger!*, which was published in 1936. Reviewing the volume, the eminent American critic Edmund Wilson commented that, for all his gifts, Auden 'seems to have been arrested at the mentality of an adolescent schoolboy'.[108] Perhaps the weakness of the texts explains the lack of impact in the musical settings. This cycle has none of the depth or power of *Our Hunting Fathers*. Britten also went on to contribute incidental music to the play *The Ascent of F6*, which Auden wrote in collaboration with his sometime lover Christopher Isherwood. A play about the questionable nature of human ambition shown in a mountaineering episode, the play premiered at the small Mercury Theatre in Ladbroke Road, Notting Hill Gate. The off-West End production was directed by Rupert Doone, who with his lover, the painter Robert Medley, ran the Group Theatre, the most progressive company in English drama in the 1930s. Doone, who began his career as a dancer in the last days of the Diaghilev company and then moved into acting and directing, was a colourful, highly temperamental figure. It is clear from Britten's diary that he did not find it easy to work with him. Nevertheless Britten's introduction into the world of theatre was to prove highly educative and indeed to be crucial in his development and achievement as a composer. Without it he surely could not have gained the dramatic skills that mark the music of the operatic masterpieces of his later years. For the introduction to Doone, to the Group Theatre and to stagecraft he was indebted to Auden.

Britten contributed the music to a later play by Auden and Isherwood, *On the Frontier*, which dealt with the Kafkaesque unrealities of modern power politics. It was first produced under the auspices of the Group Theatre and staged at the Cambridge Arts Theatre in 1938. It was not well received. As Virginia Woolf exclaimed in a letter to Vita Sackville-West: 'Lord how bad the Auden Isherwood play was!'[109] Her Bloomsbury associate John Maynard Keynes, who had helped to found the Arts Theatre, agreed. 'Unquestionably it was a failure,' he wrote to a friend. He went on to repeat a criticism of Auden and his circle that was often made: 'They are getting too old for such infantilism and amateurism.'[110]

Time has confirmed these judgements. The plays written by Britten's literary friends are long forgotten, but Britten's music of the time was a success then, as it is now. His progress as a theatre composer continued. His music came to the notice of the theatre and film producer Basil Dean, who approached Britten with a request for a substantial, variegated score to accompany *Johnson Over Jordan*, the latest play by J.B. Priestley, at the time a highly successful playwright and novelist. In its staging and themes the play was a very ambitious work. Britten was paid seventy guineas, a substantial sum to which the young composer was not at all accustomed. The play was staged at the New Theatre and subsequently at the Saville Theatre on Shaftesbury Avenue. After just a few years of supplying music for plays at fringe venues Britten had in early 1939, at the age of twenty-five, arrived at the very centre of the West End.

Basil Dean's interest in Britten's music had in part been quickened by his Piano Concerto, which had its first performance under Sir Henry Wood at the Queen's Hall on 18 August 1938. This was the occasion that marked Britten's emergence as a celebrity. When he left the famous concert hall after the performance he found a large crowd at the artists' entrance waiting to applaud him and seek his autograph. Many of the newspaper critics were far less impressed by the concerto, deploring, as in the 1930s they did with most of Britten's compositions, a lack of depth and an excess of facility and virtuosity. But the years have confirmed the judgements of the enthusiasts in that first audience. With the changes that Britten made to the third movement in 1945, the piece continues to be performed and recorded. The work is brimful of energy and high spirits and shows the infectious pleasure that the young composer takes in his very considerable musical sophistication. It is far more accessible than the, literally, more finely tuned *Our Hunting Fathers*. Readily accessible too is his *Variations on a Theme of Frank Bridge*, which was premiered just a year earlier in a performance by the Boyd Neel Orchestra at the Salzburg Festival. The references to Bridge and to performances of his music as they appear in Britten's diaries of the time make clear the unfailing esteem and respect that he felt for his long-time mentor and friend. The *Variations* carry the dedication 'To F.B. A tribute with affection and admiration'. On the composition sketch there is a list showing how each of the ten variations corresponds to what Britten saw as one of the attributes of Frank Bridge. In order of performance they are: 'His integrity, His energy, His charm, His wit, His tradition, His gaiety, His enthusiasm, His sympathy, His reverence, His skill.'[111] The title of the twelfth and final section of the work (with its significant change of pronoun adjective), 'Our

Affection', justifies itself by a highly and complicatedly wrought composition that is testimony to Bridge's teaching. The other variations are for the most part less intricate but similarly entertaining. The work was a great success at the Salzburg Festival and like the Piano Concerto has continued to receive performances. In the late 1930s the two works consolidated Britten's fast-growing reputation as a rising star.

Yet for all his quick, early successes as a composer and his fame as the wunderkind of British music, Britten's personal life was far from composure and contentment. This was so much so that by the end of the decade he had abandoned the country where he had made such a name and moved to the United States.

There appear to be several reasons for this drastic step. The political situation in Europe was increasingly dangerous and war looked probable. Britten must surely have wondered, anxiously, what would happen to him as a pacifist and a homosexual in the event of war. He was also in considerable, lingering distress as a result of the deaths in quick succession of his father and mother. His love relationships were also in some turmoil. In 1937 he had met Peter Pears, a singer with the choral group that was later to be known as the BBC Singers, and a friendship developed steadily between them. But Britten also became attracted powerfully to Wulff Scherchen, a blonde and very handsome young man in his late teens who was the son of the renowned conductor Hermann Scherchen. With money inherited from his parents Britten had bought and renovated the picturesque Old Mill at Snape, near Aldeburgh in Suffolk. Here over the Christmas period of 1938 he and Wulff finally became lovers. Wulff, who was an aspiring poet, commemorated the intensity of the experience in four simple stanzas. Britten carefully preserved the poem and carried it with him for many years:

Lost to the worlds
beyond all stars,
alone, yet one,
two beings lie.

oblivion rules
their minds, their hearts,
while tranquil there,
voluptuous, they love.

away from hate,
above all scorn,
but in their love,
they know existence.

time has no sense,
music no charms,
beauty is lost,
in lovers' frenzy.[112]

Britten, however, had qualms about maintaining the relationship with the younger man. He also learned that Peter Pears was planning what the singer envisaged as a brief stay in the United States. There is some suggestion too that Britten thought that a Hollywood producer might be interested in employing him. America offered possibilities and Auden, whom he continued at that time greatly to respect, had given a lead by himself crossing the Atlantic some time earlier. From the turmoil of newly discovered passions, uncertainties and doubts there emerged the decision to cross the Atlantic with Peter Pears.

When in April Wulff Scherchen came to visit his lover at his London flat, he found the door opening on to a boisterous farewell party for Britten and Pears. The teenager was devastated. Two weeks later Britten and Pears sailed on a Cunard White Star liner from Southampton to North America.

～

Britten's first Atlantic crossing was completed in the second week of May 1939. War looked inevitable. It was the month in which Hitler concluded his Pact of Steel with Mussolini and began his preparations for the invasion of Poland. Britten, together with Peter Pears, arrived back in England just under three years later in mid-April 1942. This was in the very middle of the Second World War, which had by then fully justified its name by becoming global. Britain, allied with the United States, was locked in a struggle with the Pact of Steel in North Africa and with the Japanese in various regions of Asia. The North Atlantic Ocean across which Britten and Pears sailed in a convoy that spring was also an important and dangerous battle area. U-boats were a serious danger to shipping and threatened the supplies of food and equipment that were vital for Britain's survival. Just a week after Britten's disembarkation at Liverpool on his return to Britain there had to be an emergency reorganization of the freighter convoys sailing from Newfoundland to Londonderry.

The period of nearly thirty-five months that Britten spent in the United States constitutes a distinct period and episode in his development as a composer. He had gone there in a state of great uncertainty. His early letters home show him living very much from week to week, month to month, as far as places to live, career plans and income were concerned. He dithered, ever more anxiously as time went by, about whether or not to return to Britain. The decision became even more problematic once the war had begun. Where he and Pears lived was decided by chance meetings, his income was unpredictable and, once war was declared and funds no longer transferable from London, sometimes painfully curtailed.

However the time Britten spent in the United States shows a rapid expansion in the range of his music. It also resulted in some important life decisions and commitments. Peter Pears, with whom he had left Britain as an amiable homosexual friend, was, on their return, established as his lover in what was to prove to be a lifelong relationship. The American years also led Britten to the clear realization that, whatever the many attractions of the United States and its musical world, England was the place to which he, unlike his friend W.H. Auden, had to commit himself and his career. He finally resolved in the middle of the war to re-cross the Atlantic, despite the many dangers of what he described to the American conductor and critic Albert Goldberg as 'that particularly nasty bit of ocean'.[113] He returned to Britain with one very specific and ambitious artistic commitment, one that was born in America and significantly helped along by American encouragement and funding: his first great opera *Peter Grimes*. The work would be the beginning, the foundation of Britten's chief achievement, his work as an opera composer. It would also inaugurate a new period and virtually a new genre in the history of English music.

Britten's stay in America broke into three very different periods. After a brief stay in Quebec, Canada, and then near Woodstock in New York State, he and Peter Pears settled in with William and Elizabeth Mayer at Amityville on Long Island. These two highly cultured émigrés from Munich had managed to find employment with Dr William Titley, a keen music lover who was Superintendent of the Long Island Home, an extensive medical facility for patients with mental health difficulties. Dr Mayer arranged for Britten and Pears to have free board and lodging within the institution and Amityville became their home for some fifteen months until November 1940. At this time the two young men moved to their second place of extended residence, a communal house at 7 Middagh Street in Brooklyn Heights, New York. February House, as the place came to be known (because so many of its occupants had February birthdays), has long since been recognized, like Andy Warhol's three Factory locations, as an important site and episode in the history of American Bohemia. Here the two English visitors lived alongside the two writers Jane and Paul Bowles and the author of the spectacularly best-selling novel *The Heart is a Lonely Hunter*, Carson McCullers. Other residents were the flamboyant George Davis, fiction editor of the venerable fashion magazine *Harper's Bazaar*, and the burlesque performer Gypsy Rose Lee, who was just then writing her detective novel *The G-String Murders*, which also was to enjoy a great success. Many other figures in the arts in New York drifted in and out for longer or shorter stays. Attempting to manage and bring order into this usually chaotic household was W.H. Auden, at whose invitation Britten and Pears had come.

They stayed in Brooklyn for some eight months, occasionally returning to Amityville for rest and recuperation. And then in June 1941 they drove all the way across America by car and began a stay of just over two months in Escondido, a small town in Southern California some thirty miles northeast of San Diego. Their hosts were the British pianists Ethel Bartlett and Rae Robertson, who had a spacious home there. Again Britten and Pears were non-paying guests. The married couple who had invited them had achieved success and prosperity as a result of their performances of the repertoire for two pianos. A generation older than Britten and Pears, they were great admirers of the young men, so much so that Ethel, a woman of carefully managed elegance (as the portraits of her painted by Harold and Laura Knight clearly demonstrate) was soon falling in love with Britten. Her husband Rae felt the gentlemanly thing was not to stand in their way. But the failure of Rae and Ethel to understand the relationship between Pears and Britten created a great deal of emotional upset among the four of them.

After they had returned to Amityville and were determining to face all the risks involved in returning to Britain, Britten told his closest confidante, his sister Beth,

> we were incredibly glad ... to get away from California – it was a lovely
> enough place, but the personal relationships got in such a deplorable mess

that any normal kind of life was impossible – and all the time we were caught up in a web of 'gratitude' since they were *paying* for us.

He concludes that he should not have accepted hospitality from such 'selfish and indulgent people ... but the temptation of staying rent-free, in such a lovely place for so long (especially as I had so much work to get done) was too much. However I have learned my lesson now, and only complain that the punishment (3 months living in an emotional volcano) was so great!'[114]

Yet to this troubled summer in California belong the origins of *Peter Grimes*. On a trip into Los Angeles Britten and Pears visited what Pears later described as a 'marvellous Rare Book Shop'. Here they came upon a one-volume edition, published in 1851, of *The Poetical Works of the Rev. George Crabbe*. At this same time they were also impressed by an article on Crabbe 's poetry by E.M. Forster, which coincidentally they discovered in a copy of *The Listener* of 29 May 1941 that had made its way to California. Forster's carefully worded characterization and commendation of the Suffolk poet and of his collection *The Borough*, arranged as twenty-four letters in heroic couplets about all aspects of the community, had a profound, career-changing effect on Britten. In a radio broadcast nearly a quarter of a century later he recalled that 'in a flash I realized two things: that I must write an opera, and where I belonged.'[115]

California it was then where Britten committed himself to opera, the musical genre in which more than any other he was to excel. More than that, *Peter Grimes* spectacularly and overnight established opera as an entity in English musical culture in a way it had never been before.

Peter Grimes was not Britten's first opera. A year before, *Paul Bunyan*, a work on which he had collaborated with W.H. Auden, had had its first performance. It was the longest work he had undertaken at Amityville, which of his three most important residences in America had seen him produce the most. Paul Bunyan was a figure belonging in the tradition of the tall tale, an important part of the folk tradition influencing American literature. Bunyan was a giant of a man, so heavy, the legend had it, that it took three storks to deliver him at birth. Among many other unbelievable feats the tall tale ascribes the creation of the Grand Canyon to Paul Bunyan, telling how he did it by allowing his great axe to drag behind him as he sauntered along with his buddy, Babe, the blue ox. Another tall tale relates how Paul, the heroic giant, ate fifty pancakes in one minute flat.

In taking up this American folk tale and attempting to bring the story forward into modern times Auden and Britten appear to have been aiming at producing a hit musical. Paul Kildea is surely right to suggest that 'from early on both men had Broadway in their sights'.[116] But neither words nor music in this piece have the pace and the punch needed for that kind of success. The work is slow, at times rambling, and the libretto is clogged by the sententiousness that affected Auden's longer works throughout his career. He readily admitted his prime responsibility for the failure of *Paul Bunyan*: 'The result, I'm sorry to say, was a failure, for which I was entirely to blame, since, at the time, I knew nothing whatsoever about opera or what is required of a librettist. In consequence some very lovely music of Britten's went down the drain.'[117] Auden and Britten would both go on to learn the crafts necessary in the opera house. Later in life Auden would create memorable texts as a librettist, most notably for Stravinsky in *The Rake's Progress* and for Hans Werner Henze in the powerful text and highly worked-out stage directions for *The Bassarids*. In several passages in the score of *Paul Bunyan* we already hear something of what was to emerge more confidently in *Peter Grimes* and the subsequent operas. It was not in Britten's musical nature to write the kind of smash-hit numbers that befit a musical. In the gentle chromaticism and the intensifying orchestral texture accompanying an aria sung by the philosopher-bookkeeper Johnny Inkslinger, however, we hear something prefiguring the subtly compelling power of Britten's mature operatic sound.

Other shorter projects instigated by Auden and completed during Britten's years in America were more successful. Not long after taking up residence with Dr and Mrs Mayer at Amityville Britten completed his song sequence *Les Illuminations*, settings of passages he had selected from Arthur Rimbaud's long poetic sequence of the same name. Auden, very probably, introduced him to this long, tumultuous work and it was one of the several instances of how the poet drastically extended Britten's literary awareness. But that Britten had a peculiarly acute receptivity, indeed susceptibility, to language, there can be no doubt. Sophie Wyss, the Swiss soprano who gave the first performance of the work, recalled Britten's intense excitement when he first read Rimbaud's sequence of mainly prose poems. She remembered that on a train journey Britten rushed up to her and spoke of his excitement at the work of the teenage French poet. He told her that he had definitely made up his mind to set some of the sections of the poem, even then deciding what passages to set and how to arrange them so as to give an architecture to the sequence.

Les Illuminations is one of the most important founding texts in the tradition of French surrealist poetry that was to thrive throughout the twentieth century. Surrealism also entered into other arts: painting, fiction, sculpture. It also moved beyond France. In England surrealism was, belatedly, to make its most visible, formal appearance in the International Surrealist Exhibition at the New Burlington Galleries in Mayfair in late June and early July 1936. The organizers included the critic Herbert Read and the sculptor Henry Moore. Among the poets attending was Dylan Thomas, whom some reviewers saw as one of Rimbaud's heirs. Very obviously working in the Rimbaud tradition was Picasso's close friend, the French poet Paul Eluard, who came to the exhibition to give a lecture entitled 'La Poésie Surréaliste'.

Surrealism was then very much a feature of the literary situation when Britten encountered *Les Illuminations*. It is a lengthy text ranging over a chaos of landscapes, cityscapes, history, characters, voices and states of consciousness. Britten displays considerable skill in his choice of passages and in assembling them. As Ian Bostridge has observed, Britten gives 'Rimbaud's prose visions a shape which, as published, they do not have – a beginning, a middle and an end.'[118] To create such a design may seem to go against the commitment to disorder, free association, automatic writing and the cult of unreason that are some of the basic assumptions of surrealist aesthetics. Britten's actual music, though, turns out to be in no way at variance with Rimbaud's fast, disconnecting, puzzling kaleidoscope of images, voices and situations. Rather it opens up, as Bostridge has put it, 'a realm of freedom and fantasy which expands into and beyond Rimbaud's linguistic virtuosity. Ferocity of invective is yoked with the humour of the flaneur and a melting sensuality of utterance making *Les Illuminations* the great masterpiece of Britten's first period.'[119]

The composer will have found the noisy chaos evoked in Rimbaud's long poem very much an equivalence for the chaos that he, like those who contributed to the International Surrealist Exhibition, saw in himself and in the world about him as he hesitatingly and without conviction set off for America. The crazy disorder of things is there in 'Towns', the second section of Britten's sequence:

These are towns! This is a people for whom these dreamlike Alleghanies and Lebanons arose. Chalets of crystal and wood move on invisible rails and pulleys. The old craters, girdled with colossi and copper palm trees, roar melodiously in the fires. Processions of Mabs in russet and opaline robes rise from the ravines. Up there, their feet in the waterfall and the brambles, the stags suckle Diana. Suburban Bacchantes sob and the moon burns and howls. Venus enters the caverns of the blacksmiths and the hermits. From groups of bell towers the ideas of the peoples sing forth. From castles built of bone the unknown music goes forth.[120]

What to many early listeners and reviewers sounded very much indeed like an 'unknown music' does in fact contain some very familiar forms. The sections entitled 'Antique' and 'Being Beauteous' are quickly recognizable as love songs. The first is addressed to Wulff Scherchen and the second to Peter Pears. In both pieces slow-moving harmonies are pushed aside as words and music evoke a sexuality that is more complicated than in most traditional love songs.

In introducing Britten to the poetry of Rimbaud Auden presented him with an inspirational gift. It seems likely that it was also Auden who introduced him to the sonnets of Michelangelo, another work involving homoerotic themes. To Enid Slater, the wife of his future literary collaborator Montagu Slater, Britten announced from Amityville in April 1940, 'I've got a sudden craze for the Michael Angelo sonnetts (*sic*) & have set about half a dozen of them (in Italian – pretty brave, but ... after Rimbaud in French I feel I can attack anything! I've got my eye on Rilke, now & Hölderlin!)'.[121] Britten never did set Rilke, though later in life he did produce his *Sechs Hölderlin Fragmente*, which is another instance of that very wide, international range of literary and musical reference that differentiates his song settings from those of Elgar and Vaughan Williams. But in 1940 in Amityville he worked away enthusiastically at what was eventually to be performed and published under the title *Seven Sonnets of Michelangelo*.

The original Italian poems were written for the great artist's beloved, the young Tommaso dei Cavalieri. As with *Les Illuminations*, Britten had come upon a text that served as a mirror for his own situation and feelings. The settings form an extended love letter celebrating his recently confirmed relationship with Peter Pears; they are carefully managed in order to suit Pears's voice. They also prefigure the opera composer of the future in that they sound like a series of small arias. And there is a great deal of contrast among them. The second piece, Sonnet XXXI, is fast moving, catching the accelerating, masochistic excitement of being taken over by love, of being the beloved's prisoner, 'prigion d'un Cavalier armato', captive of an armed cavalier. Sonnet XXX moves with a markedly contrasting slowness as the singer ponders the implications of such subordination and dependence. In Sonnet XXXVIII words and music turn querulous, bitchy even, as the speaker, feeling undervalued, asks to be set free in order that he may find an 'altra bellezza', another beauty to love. Each of the sonnets sings of a different mood in love and not all of them contented ones. But in the seventh and last, Sonnet XXIV, a profound calm is finally attained. The rising bass in the piano introduces with some formality the falling sequence of the tenor's unaccompanied 'Spirito ben nato' and then singer and accompanist at last come happily together. The piano concludes the cycle with a slow postlude rich in its expression of serene, rapt contemplation, a long lingering G major. Like *Les Illuminations*, *Seven Sonnets of Michelangelo* shows how during his years in the United States Britten's compositions moved from what some critics perceived as mere virtuosity to what are without question renderings of deeply felt experience.

At the same time that he told Enid Slater of his enthusiasm for Michelangelo, he also reported a commission that had come to him, via the British Foreign Service, from the government of Japan. What was required was a work for orchestra that would contribute to the celebrations of the 2,600th anniversary of the establishment of the Japanese Empire. But what Britten produced, the work now known as the *Sinfonia da Requiem*, was not at all what the commissioners in Tokyo had wanted and expected. A letter forwarded by the Director of the Cultural Bureau of the Japanese Foreign Office to the New York office of Britten's publishers Boosey & Hawkes regretted that 'Mr Benjamin Britten's composition is so very different from the anticipation of the Committee which had hoped to receive from a friendly nation, felicitations expressed in musical form.'[122] Britten protested but the work was finally set aside by the organizers of the celebrations in Japan. Britten who, recurrently during his years in America, was painfully short of money, did not return the substantial advance that had been paid to him.

From these peculiar, problematical circumstances there emerged another of Britten's important early works. From conception to completion the *Sinfonia da Requiem* was a work of Britten's American period, a time in his life when, apart from all the stimulus offered by the New World, he was often seriously ill, anxious financially, extremely homesick and still affected by the continuing impact of the two bereavements caused by the deaths in quick succession of his father and mother. The *Sinfonia* is dedicated to the memory of his deeply missed parents, whose lives had ended just before his decision to go to America. A profoundly felt sense of loss and guilt pervades this sombre work. But listeners have also heard the heavy, thudding funeral march that serves as an overture to the piece as a lament and commemoration for the European civilization that was to die as a result of the political calamity in which the 1930s ended. As such it is yet another counterpart to Auden's poem 'September 1939'.

The opening movement, which takes its title 'Lacrymosa' from the Latin Requiem, is the sound of a slow, oppressive cortège. The sobering, even depressing mood that it creates is scarcely alleviated by what follows, a seeming scherzo entitled 'Dies irae'. In this dance of death we now have very definitely the sounds of war, the blaring of trumpets and the strident clashings of instruments suggesting the slaughter of a battlefield. In the third and final movement, 'Requiem aeternam', the clanging cluster chords have disappeared; the music quietens and moves reflectively into a prayerful invocation of peace.

A work of less than twenty minutes duration, *Sinfonia da Requiem* is a powerful, very felt orchestral work. From the time of its first performance by the New York Philharmonic Orchestra under John Barbirolli in 1941 it attracted enthusiastic admirers in America. Among these the most influential on Britten's future career was an elderly and very wealthy Russian emigrant to the United States, Serge Koussevitzky.

In his years in America Britten made helpful contacts with many influential figures in the world of American music. Within a few months of arriving he had established a friendly relationship with the highly successful composer Aaron Copland. The creator of *Rodeo* and *Billy the Kid* was always aware that Britten, for all his deep interest in the international, modernist movement in music, retained in his own compositions qualities that showed his origins. Britten had, Copland once wrote, 'a certain forthrightness, a sense of a lyrical quality that was very British'.[123]

Another American friend and a valued patron was Elizabeth Sprague Coolidge. In her mid-seventies when Britten came into contact with her, this daughter of an extremely wealthy Chicago businessman had a long and distinguished record of supporting the work of contemporary composers, particularly in chamber music. In composing and dedicating his highly melodic String Quartet to her, Britten joined a long list of composers to whom she had given commissions, including Ravel, Prokofiev, Bartók,

Schoenberg and Copland, whose ballet *Appalachian Spring* was composed with her support.

For Britten's future career, however, and indeed for the future of English music, it was Serge Koussevitzky who was to exert the greatest and most decisive influence after the exhilarating experience of conducting *Sinfonia da Requiem* with his Boston Symphony Orchestra. This made up his mind to offer Britten a commission, specifically one for an opera.

Born in 1872, the same year as Winston Churchill, Koussevitzky achieved fame as a double bass virtuoso in his native Russia. His second wife, whose father was a successful tea merchant, inherited a vast fortune and with her backing Koussevitzky was able to found his own orchestra and set up as a music publisher. In 1920, after three years conducting the State Philharmonic Orchestra of Petrograd, he moved to Berlin and then to Paris, finally ending up in the United States, where in 1941 at he became an American citizen at the age of sixty-seven. In 1924 he had replaced Pierre Monteux as conductor of the Boston Symphony Orchestra and over nearly a quarter of a century greatly enhanced the orchestra's reputation. Britten, who was always a severe judge of orchestral performance, wrote to Elizabeth Sprague Coolidge of Koussevitzky's players that, 'I really think the orchestra is the best I have ever heard.'[124] Koussevitzky was also a prime mover in establishing the summer concert and educational programmes at Tanglewood in the western hill country of Massachusetts, an institution that was to become central to the development of music, especially modern music, in America.

Koussevitzky was quickly and greatly impressed by Britten's gifts as a composer. After conducting the *Sinfonia da Requiem* with his Boston orchestra, he complimented Britten on the dramatic power of the piece and asked him why he had not written for the opera house. Koussevitzky was perceptive enough to identify early on in Britten's career the musical genre to which the young man's genius was best suited. Britten, though, was daunted by the prospect of undertaking an opera, but when he spoke of the cost in money and time of such a risky venture, Koussevitzky promptly offered a commission. Britten then told him of Crabbe's story of Peter Grimes in *The Borough*, in which he and Peter Pears had become so keenly interested and which might be the subject for an opera. Koussevitzky approved of the idea and gave Britten one thousand dollars to help the project along. A condition of the agreement was that the work should be dedicated to Koussevitzky's wife. Years later, after the success of *Peter Grimes* in London and New York,

Koussevitzky maintained that he would have paid more had Britten asked for it.

So here was the last of several contributions that America made to the development of Britten's great creative powers. It had given him a good deal of free board and lodging and time to extend the range of his compositions and also opportunities to have them performed. It also confirmed in him, slowly but then decisively, the realization that he was, as Aaron Copland had quickly perceived, an English composer. It was the place where he had the light bulb moment in which he encountered the text that would be the origin of his distinguished career in the opera house. And in the last days of his three-year stay in America, which had taken him coast to coast, he was the recipient, from one of the greatest luminaries in American music, of the money that would help him bring his first operatic project to completion.

By the time Britten and Pears left the port of New York in the spring of 1942 they had a worked-out plot for what would become *Peter Grimes*. When they arrived back in England they would look for a librettist to produce a text. What they had in mind would make English music resound in a genre and a style that it had never produced before.

After they disembarked at Liverpool on 17 April 1942 Britten and Pears travelled down to London, where at first they stayed with relatives and friends. Quickly they began the procedure necessary for achieving (as they both finally did) acceptance and legal registration as conscientious objectors. Britten acted with similar speed in finding a writer to supply the libretto for the opera about Peter Grimes, which was now at the forefront of his thought and ambitions as a composer. Having earlier failed to interest Christopher Isherwood in the project, Britten now turned to Montagu Slater, a poet, playwright, novelist and general man of letters with whom he had at times collaborated back in the 1930s. They had worked together on the documentary film *Coal Face*; Britten also composed music for Slater's play about the Irish uprising, *Easter 1916*, which was performed in 1935, and for *Stay Down, Miner*, staged by Left Theatre the following year.

Born into a working-class family in Cumberland, Montagu Slater had won a scholarship to Magdalen College, Oxford, and begun his writing career as a journalist on the *Liverpool Post*. A convinced Marxist, he joined the Communist Party of Great Britain when he was very young and remained an unrelenting Stalinist even after the Hungarian uprising of 1956, the year at the end of which Slater died prematurely at the age of fifty-four.

On 2 May 1942, shortly after Britten and Pears returned home, the Burmese city of Mandalay fell to the Japanese. It was another in a sequence of shocks and demoralizing defeats for Britain and its then Empire, which had seen the Japanese capture the great imperial staging post of Singapore less than three months earlier. But Mandalay literally had a special resonance in British minds. The name figured in a well-known poem by Rudyard Kipling, which, set to music by Oley Speaks, had long been a favourite part of the patriotic repertoire of the music halls. The name of the city echoed in the popular mind, and now suddenly Mandalay was lost. But it was on that dark day of defeat that Britten triumphantly announced to his motherly friend Elizabeth Mayer over in America the establishment of his partnership with his communist friend in developing his opera. The three-year process of creating *Peter Grimes,* Britten's and England's first operatic masterpiece since Purcell's *Dido and Aeneas,* had begun. In the darkest days of the war the seeds of what proved to be a further stage of England's musical renewal were planted. Montagu, Britten told Elizabeth Mayer, 'has taken to Grimes like a duck to water and the opera is *leaping* ahead. It is very exciting ... he has splendid ideas.'[125] One such idea apparently was, as might be expected from a Marxist writer, to extend and emphasize the social context and conditioning of the characters in a late eighteenth-century Suffolk fishing village. 'It is', Britten continued, 'getting more and more an opera about the community, whose life is "illuminated" for this moment by the tragedy ... Ellen is growing in importance, and there are five minor characters, such as the Parson, pub-keeper, "quack-apothecary" and doctor.'

During the following summer Britten drew close to Montagu Slater and his wife Enid, who was pursuing a career as a photographer. He stayed at their home and was taken care of by them during one of the several debilitating illnesses that beset him during the war. He and Slater were very close in sympathy and understanding about the libretto. 'It is going so well', Britten reported to Elizabeth Mayer, '& I'm very keen on his whole attitude to the subject – Very simple, full of respect for Crabbe, and with real stage experience. My ideas are crystallising nicely.'[126]

Peter Grimes was the chief and continuing object of Britten's career as an artist throughout the Second World War. His realization that opera was the musical form best suited to him was steadily confirmed. And his commitment to this first major venture for the opera house was intense and single-minded. In his letters of the war years he very rarely mentions the historic events taking place in the various theatres of the worldwide conflict, but references to the progress of his opera recur continually. The result of this dedication was a masterpiece that stands besides works of similar depth produced in, and by that war: T.S. Eliot's *Little Gidding*, Francis Bacon's *Three Studies for Figures at the Base of a Crucifixion*, the lyric poems of Keith Douglas and the *Pisan Cantos* of Ezra Pound, a poet whose work Britten came very much to admire at this time.[127]

Certainly Britten undertook other compositions during the war, as well as being extremely busy as a performer. There is, for instance, his *Serenade for Tenor, Horn and Strings*, which had its first performance at the Wigmore Hall on 15 October 1943, six weeks after Italy had capitulated and the war at last showed signs of turning in favour of the Allies. For this work Britten returned to English lyric poetry, setting pieces by, among others, Blake, Tennyson and Ben Jonson. This last section is a memorable, thrilling duet for tenor voice and horn played at that first performance by Dennis Brain, the horn player who had first asked that Britten write such a piece.

Britten also responded to a request from that singular art patron of the war period, the Reverend Walter Hussey, vicar of St Matthew's, Northampton. A fervent believer in the value of the arts in the life of the Church, Hussey worked tirelessly to bring new art to his provincial parish. He commissioned a *Crucifixion* from the painter Graham Sutherland, a festival anthem, *Lo, the full, final sacrifice*, from Gerald Finzi and what was to become a renowned work of sculpture, a *Madonna and Child* from Henry Moore. Out of the blue Hussey approached Britten for a piece to help commemorate the fiftieth anniversary of the consecration of St Matthew's, built as a memorial to a prosperous brewer. It was agreed that Britten would set another English text, Christopher Smart's poem *Jubilate Agno*. The resulting cantata for soprano, alto, tenor and bass soloists, together with choir and organ, turned out to be a work with a distinctly operatic character. Written while the improvident author was the inmate of a private madhouse in Bethnal Green, Smart's poem, especially in the section 'For I will consider my Cat Jeoffry', is a celebration of God's creation and especially animal creation. Britten's fifteen-minute piece well conveys Smart's delight and joyousness. Like the *Serenade*, the cantata serves to remind the war-weary of heartening realities that offer a diversion from the demoralizing horrors of the war.

But these smaller works were incidental to Britten's chief creative concern during the war, his opera. Here on his own terms and through his evolving music he contemplated violence, destructiveness, human suffering and loss. Five months after his return to Britain he pronounced 'the opera libretto … finished (and excellent too)'.[128] In the event the text was to undergo several more revisions and redactions, but Britten's announcement shows how much he continued (as he had from the very start) to be involved in the verbal and dramaturgical components of *Peter Grimes*. Britten was a composer with considerable literary knowledge and ability. He was also keenly aware that an opera is far more than its music.

As the next few months went by, however, Britten's confidence in what had been created faltered. These were still uncertain days. In March 1943, just after the biggest German submarine attack ever in the mid-Atlantic, in which twenty-one cargo ships were sunk by the U-boat wolf pack, Britten, suffering badly from a case of chickenpox, confided his new doubts and uncertainties about his opera to Peter Pears. He was going, he wrote,

> to do lots of work on P. Grimes today, to see what really is wrong with it. And then I shall write a long letter to Montagu & hope he can fix it abit (*sic*). I am sure it isn't *fundamentally* hopeless, there are too many things to like about it. For one thing it goes *naturally* into operatic form – it doesn't embarrass me to think of those people, singing, & singing English. And another, I see so clearly what kind of music I want to write for it, & I am interested in the people & the situations, & interested in a musical way.[129]

His lurking uncertainty even led him to question Montagu Slater's suitability as the literary collaborator to set the opera to rights: 'I'm beginning to feel that Montagu may not be the ideal librettist.' He pondered replacements, mentioning Auden and Louis MacNeice, but concluded that neither would be a good choice.

By the following day Britten seemed to have started to find his way through the difficulties with the text and the characterization of the fisherman who is the central figure of the opera. To Erwin Stein, one of the editorial group at Boosey & Hawkes, he wrote,

> one bit of good work I'm doing is on the opera libretto – I am finding lots of possibilities of improvement, especially the character of Grimes himself

which I find doesn't come across clearly enough. At the moment he is just a pathological case – no reasons & not many symptoms. He's got to be changed alot. But even then, I am convinced that it is right for me to do *this* opera. I am too interested in it for me to drop it now.'[130]

Work on the improvements seems to have gone well and by the end of 1943 there was no longer any question about Montagu's standing as the librettist. Britten told Elizabeth Mayer that, 'The friends we see most of now are Enid and Montagu Slater (his libretto is excellent now).' Nevertheless a couple of months later he told Ralph Hawkes that he was still not satisfied with the text: 'The opera is going well but I am making enormous changes all the while in the libretto.'[131]

As he continued his tortuous struggle to work on *Peter Grimes* over this long time span, always feeling himself inextricably committed to the project, Britten had a strong sense of being in the grip of the zeitgeist, of being implicated in a profound change in the temper of the times. It was an awareness he discovered he shared with an unexpected admirer, Imogen Holst, who was associated in his mind with a group at the Royal College of Music that he believed to be unfriendly to him. In a letter to her that provides an interesting perspective on the times in which *Peter Grimes* was created, Britten wrote,

It is also encouraging that you too sense that 'something' in the air which heralds a renaissance. I feel terrifically conscious of it, so do ... so many that I love & admire – it is good to add you to that list! Whether we are the voices crying in the wilderness or the thing itself, it isn't for us to know, but anyhow it is so very exciting. It is of course in all the arts, but in music, particularly, it's this acceptance of 'freedom' without any arbitrary restrictions, this simplicity, this contact with the audiences of our own time, & of people like ourselves.[132]

This feeling, as both man and composer, of being involved in a historical moment intensified during the following months. In a letter written just a couple of months after the D-Day landings in Normandy and a fortnight after an abortive assassination attempt on Adolf Hitler, Peter Pears wrote to a friend in America about the perception shared by so many – of an English music newly resounding:

We have the feeling here that in these dark times the seed is slowly growing. English music is really appearing again as music and itself, free of old nostalgias and preconceptions with non-musical ideas. I do so long for you to know all of them and share our vitality and confidence and, in spite of everything, gaiety.[133]

The genre that brought gaiety into Britten's life was opera, a genre of which he was now earning a closer knowledge. As he continued his work on *Peter Grimes* he commented to Peter Pears that, 'I don't know whether I shall ever be a good opera composer, but it's wonderful fun to try.'[134] In that same letter he reported problems in composition that we now know that he solved brilliantly:

I have been at it for two days solidly and got the greater part of the Prologue done. It is very difficult to keep the amount of recitative moving without going round and round in circles, I find – but I think I've managed it. It is also difficult to keep it going fast and yet paint moods and characters abit (*sic*).

He concluded the letter with the confident and prescient statement, 'P.G.'s going to be a knock-out!'[135]

By 10 March 1944, as military preparations for the D-Day landings in France intensified, particularly in southern England, Britten could say that the musical scoring for *Peter Grimes* was complete. There remained the question of where the opera might be accepted and staged. Here surely Britten's close relationship with Peter Pears, for whom he had written the title role, was helpful, for during the war years, while Britten had persevered in becoming an opera composer, Peter Pears had pursued an increasingly successful career as an opera singer. Within weeks of returning from America he had managed to obtain the title role in a production of Offenbach's *The Tales of Hoffmann* put on at the Strand Theatre in London by the short-lived Albion Opera Company. He was a great success and was soon singing principal roles for the more established Sadler's Wells Company. With their London theatre in Rosebery Avenue requisitioned by the army, the ensemble had become peripatetic. Pears quickly became one of their regular performers, singing leading roles in *La traviata*, *The Bartered Bride* and *Così fan tutte*. Pears was in fact extremely busy, if not overworked, during the war as he travelled about taking opera to venues throughout the country. He also came to know such influential figures in the world of opera as the director Tyrone Guthrie and the soprano and administrator Joan Cross.

Britten submitted the opera to Sadler's Wells Company and on 26 August 1944, just a fortnight before the first V2 rockets fell on London, he was able to tell a friend that, 'The opera went down well with the "powers" at Sadlers (*sic*) Wells and most arrangements are now complete for the production.'[136] But even now there was to be yet one more hesitation and one further major redaction of words and music. Once again Britten became dissatisfied with the version he thought he had brought to completion with Montagu Slater. He now turned to the twenty-nine-year-old Eric Crozier, who had learned his theatre craft as an apprentice at the Old Vic and worked in the BBC television drama department on some of their early productions before the war. He then became a member of the Sadler's Wells ensemble, working for and with Joan Cross, who had been a pupil of Gustav Holst and became the director of the Wells company in the early 1940s. Crozier was chosen to be the director of *Peter Grimes*. He worked well with Britten, who found him 'intelligent and clear-sighted',[137] and together they made various improvements to the opera.

Another figure to whom Britten turned in his final uncertainties about his opera was a literary friend from the 1930s, Ronald Duncan. A pacifist and close associate of the American poet Ezra Pound, Duncan had written the words for Britten's *Pacifist March*. Without involving Montagu Slater, Britten travelled to Duncan's house in North Devon and together they worked on some final changes, including a considerable enhancement of the passage in which Grimes appears to be losing his reason. On his return to London Britten reported confidentially to Duncan that, 'Montagu agreed to the new mad-scene, & I kept your part in it fairly quiet, altho' I murmured that you helped us abit (*sic*). Actually your work in that omens well for our future work together, I think.'[138] This last sentence was to be confirmed by events because when Britten, enthused by the resounding success of *Peter Grimes*, quickly set about writing another opera, *The Rape of Lucretia*, Ronald Duncan was his choice for writing the libretto.

In that historic June of 1945, however, it was the colleagues at the newly reopened Sadler's Wells Theatre with whom Britten was most intensely and excitedly involved. The success of that first night was an historic occasion in the annals of the arts in Britain. The first night of John Osborne's *Look Back in Anger* at the Royal Court Theatre on 8 May 1956 is often remembered as a major turning point for English theatre, but the play was neither the inherent masterpiece nor the foundation of a new art form in England that *Grimes* proved to be.

Joan Cross, who sang the role of Ellen Orford on that celebrated first night, recalled some twenty years later her feelings and impressions, standing on stage after the curtain came down. Above all she was struck by the quality of playing by the orchestra under the direction of Reginald Goodall. Older than most of the other principal figures in the production, Goodall must have been out of sympathy with their generally left-wing views and motives for he himself had been a member of Sir Oswald Mosley's British Union of Fascists and a Nazi sympathizer of many years standing. Nevertheless Joan Cross was in no doubt about his achievement in conducting Britten's opera: 'One thing I'm sure of and that is the high quality of the orchestra playing. They were probably a very moderate band individually, but that night they pulled out all the stops for Reggie Goodall and I count him the supreme *Grimes* conductor.'[139]

She was also struck by the utter silence that followed the ending of the first performance. The singers on stage, preparing to take their bow, were nervous and uncertain about what the silence meant. But then

> shouting broke out. The stage crew were stunned: they thought it was a demonstration. Well, it was but fortunately it was of the right kind. My main memory was of being given a great bowl of waterlilies by Peter and Ben which I took straight off to the Savoy. Why waterlilies? Well, they were original, weren't they? Everything Peter and Ben did was original.

History has confirmed Britten's own surmise about that first night. To his future close collaborator Imogen Holst he wrote, 'I think the occasion is actually a greater one than either Sadler's Wells or me, I feel. Perhaps it is an omen for English Opera in the future.'[140]

〰

The immediate and spectacular success of *Peter Grimes* confirmed Britten in a realization that opera, more than any other, was to be his special genre of music. It proved to be the one in which he created his finest, most profound achievements as a composer and the one in which he enriched, in an unprecedented way, the history of serious music in England.

He took up this new commitment rapidly and energetically. In little over two years following the first night of *Peter Grimes* he had composed and staged two more full-length operas and created what was essentially his own opera company, the English Opera Group. In his letters he would habitually write of opera in highly serious, even reverential terms. When, for instance, he first looked through early drafts of *The Rake's Progress*, when that work was being created by his friend Auden in collaboration with Stravinsky, he exclaimed to friends,

> I feel miserably disappointed (I have done since I first saw the libretto & first pages of the score) that easily the greatest composer alive should have such an irresponsible and perverse view of opera (of the voice & of the setting of words and of characterisation in particular). Of course I am sure it will contain lots of beautiful music ... but I'm not yet convinced that it helps opera to keep alive one little bit.[141]

In this last sentence the word 'opera' clearly has for Britten the connotations of an endangered institution and of a cause. And so it was to be for him during the immediate post-war years. His response was to do his utmost to create another major work in the genre. Up to the time of the Festival of Britain in 1951, throughout the years of austerity, his masterpiece *Billy Budd* came to dominate his creative career in the same way that *Peter Grimes* had done during the war years.

But first, during the time when he was schooling himself in his preferred musical genre and pondering the historical forms of opera, he attempted something that reminds us of the *opera seria* of the eighteenth century and before: *The Rape of Lucretia*. It seems to have been a hasty job. Evidence suggests that this first opera to follow *Peter Grimes* was composed, rehearsed and performed in less than seven months. A week before Christmas 1945 Britten reported to his publisher Ralph Hawkes, 'I haven't started the Rape of Lucretia yet, but Ronnie Duncan is half-way thro' the libretto which I think terrific.'[142] On this occasion Britten's usually perceptive literary judgement lets him down, for Ronald Duncan's extremely wordy, at times unintelligible text is one of the features of the opera that excludes it from the list of Britten's major works for the opera house.

The text sets the story of the rape of the virtuous Roman wife Lucretia by the passionate, headstrong King Tarquin within the context of a narrative spoken in the present by a modern male and female chorus. They assess the crime from a contemporary, Christian point of view. The text belongs very audibly in that period of poetic drama, now for the most part forgotten, that dominated the serious West End theatre in the late 1940s and early 1950s. Abandoning the speech of the middle classes that was reproduced in the plays of their immediate predecessors, such as Somerset Maugham, Noël Coward, J.B. Priestley and Terence Rattigan, the practitioners of poetic drama employed a highly wrought, verbally enriched language that removed the characters and audience from the austere realities of the day. Poetic drama in twentieth-century England had its most readily discernible origin in *Murder in the Cathedral,* a verse account of the assassination of Thomas Becket at Canterbury. It was the work of Ronald Duncan's publisher, T.S. Eliot. After its first staging in the chapter house of Canterbury Cathedral in June 1935, the production transferred to the Mercury Theatre in Notting Hill Gate where it had a successful run of 225 performances. (This was the same venue where Auden's plays, sometimes accompanied by music by Britten, were staged.) A year later Eliot's play was one of the first to be performed on the BBC's newly inaugurated television service. After the war poetic drama was continued, most successfully by Christopher Fry. The first of his sequence of plays that had great success in the West End was *The Lady's Not for Burning,* a work reminiscent of Shakespeare's pastoral comedies, which had an extended run at the Globe Theatre (now the Gielgud). Fry's prominence in the West End was maintained by plays such as *Venus Observed* and *The Dark is Light Enough,* which opened in 1954 featuring incidental music by Leonard Bernstein. Two years later *Look Back in Anger* was performed at the Royal Court Theatre and an entirely new mode of theatre began.

Verse drama depends for its effectiveness on the quality of its language and none of these plays of the 1940s and '50s has the linguistic quality to make them much remembered today, with the exception of Dylan Thomas's radio play *Under Milk Wood,* broadcast posthumously in 1954. Their language is characteristically verbose and often pretentious, and unfortunately for Britten this was the case with the libretto of *The Rape of Lucretia.* It contrasts markedly with the terseness, trenchancy and memorability of the Montagu Slater text for *Peter Grimes.* Like several of Fry's successful plays, the libretto Britten had to work with was based on a French original, the verbally economical *Le Viol de Lucrèce* by André Obey. But Duncan's text goes way beyond this original by introducing difficult issues of guilt and redemption broached in the language of ethics and theology. They are of a complexity that does not belong in the opera house

After setting *The Rape of Lucretia* and attempting to cater to contemporary literary taste, Britten, still fired by his newly discovered and released passion for opera, immediately turned to the writing of another. In this he was far more successful. Eric Crozier, the man of the theatre who had directed *Peter Grimes*, suggested as a good prospect for an opera another French text, Guy de Maupassant's novella *Le Rosier de Madame Husson*, translated as 'Madame Husson's May King'. Here was an opportunity to create a piece of still another sort, a comic opera. Britten happily agreed to the idea and Crozier set to work. Three months after the premiere at Glyndebourne of *The Rape of Lucretia* he was able to tell Britten that the libretto of what was to be entitled *Albert Herring* was 'roughly knocked into shape'. He had transposed the setting of the story from Normandy to Luxford, a small town in Suffolk. The action begins with a prominent figure of the locality deliberating on the choice of a May Queen for their annual spring festival. Each of the local maidens is eliminated on the grounds of questionable conduct with young men. The committee has to resort to a young man to be May King instead. The choice is Albert Herring, the quiet and simple son of a domineering mother who runs the grocery shop. At the party celebrating Albert's coronation the white-suited king unknowingly drinks lemonade that has been spiked with rum. The culprit is Sid, the butcher's boy who is in love with the attractive, kindly Nancy and who is far more worldly about men and women than timid, repressed Albert. Somewhat intoxicated, Albert flees the confines of Luxford and his bullying mother and, spending some of the money awarded to him as May King at various pubs, becomes quite drunk and gets into fights in nearby villages. The wreath with which he had been crowned is found the next day lying in the road and crushed by a passing cart. The townspeople are grief-stricken and join in a great threnody expressing their new and shocked understanding of the axiom that 'In the midst of life is death'. There is in this extended passage an irony similar to that attaching to 'Soave sia il vento', the great trio in the first act of Mozart's *Così fan tutte*, when the two heroines, Dorabella and Fiordiligi, joined by the cynical manipulator Don Alfonso, sing sadly and lovingly of their hopes that the wind and waves will smile upon their two departing suitors, whose return from a military campaign is uncertain. The trio, if we discount Don Alfonso, is the music of the deceived and so is the great ensemble near the end of *Albert Herring* for, as the community mourns, the May King suddenly returns, dishevelled and unrepentant. The townspeople reproach him, particularly for causing his mother much pain. But Albert is unmoved. It was her fault for smothering him and preventing him from expressing himself.

In his autobiography *Hallelujah Junction*, John Adams, Britten's most obvious immediate successor as a major composer of opera in English, said that, 'I am astonished at how rarely the unison of music and text succeeds in English language opera.' He goes on to note that 'People invariably point to Benjamin Britten as the gold standard of setting texts in English.'[143] This view was very much shared by Britten's librettist at the time of collaborating with him on *Albert Herring*. Eric Crozier told his wife-to-be Nancy Evans, who sang the part of the sensuous Nancy on the opening night, that Britten's 'setting of words is remarkable; he transforms them in a curious way, and it's very fascinating when the words are one's own, like seeing them suddenly in colour after black and white.'[144] Certainly Britten's music in this opera gives a brightness, sparkle and charm to a story that in plot summary could seem like something that might have been a comedy produced by Ealing Studios at this time. But in performance this comic opera, gently propelled by its music, maintains pace and interest. It is witty, unassuming music that gently mocks the opera's characters: the bumbling, well-meaning vicar, the stiffly pompous policeman and the bullying local grandee Lady Billows, characterized by a parodic version of the patriotic strains of Elgar. *Albert Herring* is carried along by amusing allusive music that makes pleasing comic reference to other opera composers and situations: when Sid laces Albert's soft drink Britten cites the love-potion motif in Wagner's *Tristan und Isolde*. Echoes of Verdi also run through the comedy, culminating in the music of the great ensemble towards the end. This memorable passage touches on an ambivalence that attaches to the purple passages in many an opera. The audience is simultaneously impressed by the power of the music but nevertheless definitely aware that the emotions expressed are rhetorically overstated or misplaced or merely a pretext for a good musical display. Britten had a strong intuitive sense of the essential nature of opera and its traditions.

Albert Herring had its premiere on 20 June 1947 at Glyndebourne, the country opera house in East Sussex that had been built by the wealthy landowner John Christie. The festival had opened in 1934 with *Le nozze di Figaro* and *Così fan tutte*, followed in later seasons by more Mozart, *Don Pasquale* and Verdi's *Macbeth*. But the relationship between Britten and his hosting impresario was extremely uneasy. This was in part because the two men had different aims for opera in England and in part because of the considerable financial losses incurred by a provincial tour of *The Rape of Lucretia*, which Christie had underwritten. The tense situation helped confirm Britten in his resolve to take a further step in the world of opera: to create his own opera company. His was the chief initiative in the founding of the English Opera Group.

The decision was announced in a statement made by Britten's associate in the venture, Eric Crozier, the librettist of *Albert Herring*. In a letter to John Christie, Crozier confirmed that

> After consideration Ben and I have reached this decision. We intend immediately to set up a non-profit-making company of our own, and to collect private capital for the launching of our next season ... The new company will be administered by a Board of Directors. Ben and I will serve as joint executive managers, and we shall appoint a General Manager to handle all our financial affairs.[145]

The new company proceeded to take *Albert Herring* on the road, first to Amsterdam where they performed it in conjunction with *The Rape of Lucretia*. They then moved on to Lucerne. And so began, ambitiously, the venture that was to take up so much of Britten's time and energy in travelling, conducting and composing during the following years. Britten committed himself to the new opera company with fervour. He enthused to Ralph Hawkes,

> I am passionately interested in it – I am keen to develop a new art form (the chamberopera, or what you will) which will stand beside the grand opera as the quartet stands beside the orchestra. I hope to write many works for it, & to be interested in this company for many years ... I am passionately keen that the continent will see what we in England can do ... & also to see what this new kind of opera can accomplish.[146]

With Britten, as with Vaughan Williams and Elgar, there was a steady, continuing determination to prove the worth and independence of English music in the face of that produced on 'the continent'.

From now on the new company and the very English opera it was established to create dominated Britten's creative concerns. Opera in its many aspects was now his métier. Above all it was his prime focus as a composer. In the years immediately following the establishment of the English Opera Group he produced non-operatic compositions, most notably the *Spring Symphony*, which had been commissioned some time before by his faithful backer over in America, Serge Koussevitzky. But opera possibilities for his company were at the forefront of his compositional ambitions.

From the start, however, the finances of the company were precarious and in time they were to become a cause of serious anxiety for Britten. It was surely in a search for a popular, money-making success for the company that he turned, after *Albert Herring*, to that very early hit in the history of English opera, John Gay's *The Beggar's Opera* of 1728. He must have been aware that a version of this great national favourite had enjoyed a memorably successful run of 1463 performances at the Lyric Theatre, Hammersmith, from June 1920. This spectacular box office achievement was a version of Gay's original (itself an anthology of extant popular tunes) put together by the successful singer Frederic Austin, who had another hit back in 1909 when he published an arrangement of 'The Twelve Days of Christmas'.

But if Britten hoped his new arrangement of *The Beggar's Opera* would have the reception Austin had enjoyed, and a financial success that would help to stabilize his struggling opera company, his plan did not work out. Well received by the reviewers at its first performance by the English Opera Group at the Cambridge Arts Theatre, Britten's arrangement and reworking of the piece were never the outstanding success with theatregoers that he appears to have aimed for. His version downplays readily singable melodies and instead offers more sophisticated fare: simple melodies done in canon form, a John Gay solo transformed into a rich ensemble, surprising folk-fiddle accompaniments to some of the well-known and well-loved songs. Although seeming to emulate the Austin version, Britten also appears to be reacting against it. In the programme for the Cambridge production he wrote:

> The tunes to which John Gay wrote his apt and witty lyrics are among our finest national songs. These seventeenth and eighteenth century airs, known usually as 'traditional tunes', seem to me to be the most characteristically *English* of any of our folksongs. They are often strangely like Purcell and Handel ... but I feel that most recent arrangements have avoided their toughness and strangeness, and have concentrated only on their lyrical prettiness.[147]

As the mention of Purcell and Handel indicated, Britten's version of *The Beggar's Opera* was not merely intended as a money-spinner for the English Opera Group, it was also an opportunity for Britten to ponder the theatre music that derived from the century of two great early masters of English opera.

That proselytizing for the musical form to which he had become so intensely and studiously dedicated was clearly present in the next project he completed, *Let's Make an Opera*, a work devised to interest children. Written in the spring of 1949, the piece was completed in just three weeks and the composing gave him great pleasure. Eric Crozier commented, 'I have seldom seen Ben so cheerful as he is these days. He is loving writing the children's opera and goes about with a beaming smile ... [The piece is] as simple as can be and great fun.'[148]

Simple it is. The first half is a little play written by Crozier in which amateur performers set about writing and rehearsing an opera. As with *The Young Person's Guide to the Orchestra* (1946), this opening seeks to explain and to make attractive and accessible an art form that in the late 1940s was generally seen as even more elitist and unreachably remote from most lives than it is now. The second half of the show is the one-act opera in three scenes that has been worked out in the opening part. Set in the year 1810 and entitled *The Little Sweep*, the opera is based on William Blake's poem 'The Chimney Sweeper'. In Britten's version it is very much a children's story in which well-to-do children in a mansion, Iken Hall, eventually manage to rescue the little chimney sweep boy Sammy, who is being used, bullied and exploited by Black Bob and his son Clem, 'a sullen apprentice as black as his dad'. It all ends happily of course with one of the four songs in which the audience is invited to join in the singing. We are given in miniature a grand finale reminiscent of grand opera. Sammy is smuggled into a trunk that is hauled away in a coach, while the successful young plotters arrange a rocking horse and chairs to provide a setting for a highly melodious mime celebrating Sammy's escape into freedom.

Let's Make an Opera was a slight and brief diversion within the three-and-a-half-year period in which Britten worked steadily on his next serious and highly ambitious work for the opera stage, his second masterpiece *Billy Budd*. In this his literary co-worker would be someone who was, and still is, recognized as one of the greatest writers of the time. In July 1948 Britten told a friend that E.M. Forster would collaborate with him 'on the next opera'. Eric Crozier was also to be involved in the project. Initially there was uncertainty about what text was to be set. But by November that year, two months after flogging, a subject in the opera, was abolished as legal punishment in the United Kingdom, it seems that the three had decided to set *Billy Budd, Foretopman*. This was the title then given to the unfinished novella that was the last work of fiction by the nineteenth-century American writer Herman Melville.

From Britten's correspondence it is clear that Forster quickly took over from Crozier the prime responsibility in preparing the libretto. By March 1949 Britten reported to Ralph Hawkes from his recently acquired house by the sea in the middle of the Suffolk fishing village of Aldeburgh: 'The libretto is astonishing. Forster has been staying here for the last three weeks and has sketched out practically the complete work. He is at the height of his form and most people will consider that that is without rival today.' Britten goes on to make clear that Eric Crozier's role in the new project was very much an ancillary one. 'Eric has been helping considerably and has in fact done all the research into naval behaviours of 1797 – a considerable subject.'[149] Forster's literary powers, we can now see, far exceeded those of any of Britten's other librettists. Crozier himself readily acknowledged this. Observing Forster's developing libretto of *Billy Budd* he commented, 'watching Morgan at work has shown me how hair-splittingly exact a good writer must be. It is hard to combine natural exuberance and fussiness in the right proportions, but I hope eventually to find a true balance.'[150]

But Crozier did not have the opportunity to perfect his craft on this particular enterprise. By the summer of 1949 financial difficulties forced him to start distancing himself from the impecunious English Opera Group and he appears to have had minimal involvement in the finalizing of the text. In late July of that year Britten told a friend, 'After this week I settle down with Morgan to finishing the Billy Budd libretto. So far what he's done is superb. He has a wonderful natural sense of the theatre, & his crisp pregnant dialogue will be good to set, I think.'[151]

And how right he was! *Billy Budd* is a fine example of the twofold expressiveness, words and music, which is opera. On so many occasions in this opera words and music endorse and enhance each other most tellingly. The text that Forster completed for Britten is a rich one. It speaks on at least three levels. There is the story of a shipboard animosity that leads to confrontation, violence, murder and an occasion of conspicuous injustice. The text simultaneously endows this drama with a metaphysical significance. The persecution of the honest, biddable and well-meaning young sailor, Billy Budd, by the profoundly cynical and malicious Master-at-Arms, John Claggart, quickly leads us into difficult abstractions such as good and evil. At the end of the opera another problematical concept has emerged, that of redemption. In Billy's last, and very important, powerful aria there is a passage that tilts towards Christian metaphysics as Billy, in modest homely terms, sees a similarity between his own acceptance of self-sacrifice that initiates redemption and that of another young man, Jesus Christ. Such a reference seems likely to have been prompted by Britten himself, whose Christian sympathies were more pronounced than was the case with the sometimes militant humanist E.M. Forster.

A third level of meaning in the libretto is one which the author of *Howard's End* and *A Passage to India* had pondered a great deal; this has to do with politics and history. The opera is set in the year 1797, in the midst of the wars with Napoleon, the inheritor of the French Revolution. The political ideas and ideals of that revolution are a major reference in the text. Billy Budd, the homely, uneducated young sailor has been press-ganged and kidnapped from a merchant ship called *Rights o' Man* and forcibly brought aboard HMS *Indomitable*. This British man-o'-war, which operates in the service of the monarchical and reactionary forces of the day, is captained by the thoughtful, well-read and well-meaning Edward Fairfax Vere. The names of the two ships and the differing musical motifs that attach to them allude to the political themes of the opera. *Rights o' Man* is named for the highly influential book by Thomas Paine published in two parts in 1791 and 1792, some seven years or so before the events presented in *Billy Budd*. The book formulated and promoted the principles of the French Revolution. It was a riposte to another famous volume of political thought, Edmund Burke's classic statement of conservative principles, *Reflections on the Revolution in France*. Paine argues in favour of democracy, the abolition of aristocratic ranks and titles, lower taxes for the poor and the provision of free education for all. *Rights of Man* quickly established itself as a basic text for progressive thought throughout the western world. In the opera, when the ship named for the book is mentioned the musical motif is rousing and inspiriting. The young, hopeful and ambitious Billy Budd comes from that world of new, humane possibilities.

He finds himself imprisoned, however, on HMS *Indomitable*, a brutal institution of the *ancien régime* in which the human rights of the forcibly conscripted sailors are scornfully disregarded by the likes of John Claggart.

Only an American writer such as Herman Melville could have written such a damning exposure of life in the Royal Navy, an institution that was idealized and romanticized in English song and story throughout the nineteenth century, for example in Stanford's *Songs of the Fleet*. The sailors of the *Indomitable* exist in perpetual fear of a shameful, humiliating flogging. Human dignity on this English warship is set at nought. The name of the ship boasts of military invincibility, but also suggests something unrelenting and atavistic that the innovative ideas and policies of thinkers like Tom Paine cannot conquer. The music of the opening scene with its heavy rhythms powerfully establishes the dehumanizing, deadening routine to which the sailors on this ship, a metaphor for the larger world, are compelled to submit.

'Oh heave! Oh heave away, heave! Oh heave!' These are the words the chorus of sailors continue to repeat. The first occasion of their singing them is accompanied by a stage direction indicating that the first mate 'hits one man a crack with a rope's end'. This establishes right from the outset the brutality that is the custom on board the *Indomitable*. As the one line sung by the chorus returns and returns, the sense of oppression mounts, Britten's orchestral accompaniment stressing the grinding, dehumanizing rhythms of the ship's rituals.

And yet by the end of the first scene the choral music has changed markedly and dramatically. More powerful than the weary resignation and the sullen anger created by the bullying exploitation are the feelings of patriotism and admiration inspired by the sight of Captain Vere. A pronounced contrast to that opening dirge-like music is the throb of enthusiasm that enters into the sailors' voices as they sing:

Long live our Captain!
Here's to our Navy!
Long live the Sovereign!
God bless our enterprise!
We're proud to serve you, Starry Vere!

This is one of the passages that were removed when the original four-act version of 1951 was condensed into a two-act edition in 1960 and so does not appear in all recordings.

The profound contradiction established, both verbally and musically, in this opening section is one of many such in the opera. The most important, for both plot and theme, is that between the good-hearted, ingenuous Billy, endowed with the tonality of B flat major, and the embittered Claggart, characterized by B minor, who schemes to compromise and destroy him. The upshot is that Claggart brings about his own destruction and death as well as Billy's. He is akin to the Mephistopheles of Goethe's *Faust*, the spirit that always denies, that believes that everything that comes into being is worthy only of its own destruction.

In his two most considerable novels, *Howard's End* and *A Passage to India*, Forster had carefully investigated such profound dualities. In the first of these the deep divisions he portrays in Edwardian England between the social classes, between men and women, between Liberals and Conservatives, and between social conscience and social complacency, prove to be not clearly resolvable in political terms. The essentially political question at the thematic centre of *Howard's End* – who shall inherit England? – is at the last referred not to human action but to a metaphysical, more specifically a mystical entity represented by the ancient tree in the garden of Howard's End. In *A Passage to India*, which portrays, often in terms of fine comedy, even more divisions than appear in *Howard's End*, the visionary also becomes part of the narrative and serves as the ultimate thematic recourse. This is shown in the episode at the Marabar Caves, where Mrs Moore, the pre-eminent representation of conciliation, is mentally and emotionally violated by the implication of the terrifying echo. It reduces all human speech, words and categories to one and the same and, most horrifyingly, to nothing. Here is another version of the spirit that always denies. The novel continues on after Mrs Moore dies, but that ultimate metaphysical question that confronted and finally destroyed her is also a cause of the gentle scepticism that informs Forster's authorial tone throughout the novel.

In *Billy Budd*, too, the various destructive conflicts present in this narrative, the claims and struggle for the rights of man, for instance, are shown not to be susceptible to solution on a social or political level. They are tacitly referred to a higher and mystical level of being. At one point in the opera Billy's admiring shipmates offer to support him in a rebellion against the order that has so unjustly brought him to disaster and imminent death. But mutiny and revolution are not for him. Such political acts are no answer, no solution. The only political act of which Billy is capable, and that unconsciously, is his last, very extended aria. Here he modestly and uncomplainingly accepts the status quo of the *Indomitable*, including his own death sentence and fate. He pardons the captain who conceivably had it within his powers to save him and, as his final words on earth, sings 'Starry Vere, God bless you!' Thematically crucial in this extended aria is what comes next: Billy's modestly worded and completely unpretentious assertion of the goodness that exists in human beings. The carefully managed verbal power and the musical conviction of such a statement are for Britten and Forster all that art can offer in the face of the destructive conflicts that this opera confronts.

The epilogue, which concludes the piece and in which Captain Vere, many years later, reviews his questionable role in the killing of Billy Budd, contains passages that remember, refer to and quote Billy's final aria but with a lower intensity. Vere for all his wide reading and his many years of experience here sounds bumbling and uncertain. Hearing Vere we inevitably remember what has just gone before in the opera. His words and music, the words and music of inadequacy, offer a contrast that illuminates and extends the power of Billy's declaration. The words that Forster gives to Billy and the music with which Britten authenticates them are a simple, confident and convincing assertion of goodness as part of the reality of what is indomitable in the world. Billy's concluding aria is one of the great passages in the opera of the twentieth century.

∾

An important place of origin for opera in one important early strain of its development was the palace of kings or the mansion of aristocrats. In its early history it was a court art form and entertainment. Through a coincidence Britten in the early 1950s was to revert to that tradition when he was commissioned to write an opera to serve as part of the celebration of a grand monarchical occasion, the Coronation of Queen Elizabeth II. The coincidence was that his eligibility for this task was in part established through his accidental acquaintance and friendship with the Queen's cousin, Lord Harewood.

At the time of his birth in 1923, nearly ten years after that of Benjamin Britten, the Hon. George Lascelles was sixth in line of succession to the British throne. As Viscount Lascelles he had an eventful career as a junior Grenadier Guards officer during the Second World War in which he was wounded, taken prisoner and, on Hitler's express orders, given a death warrant. The order was ignored by the SS Commandant of his prisoner-of-war camp who released him to the neutral Swiss. On his return to Britain he succeeded his father as 7th Earl of Harewood in 1947 and worked at court, serving intermittently as a Counsellor of State, assisting first his uncle King George VI and then his cousin Queen Elizabeth II. Lord Harewood was also a keen music enthusiast with a special interest in opera. In 1950 he launched the magazine *Opera*, which he edited until 1953. From 1951 to 1953 he was also Director of the Royal Opera House, Covent Garden, resuming the position for three more years in 1969. He was also very much involved with English National Opera and with what began as its touring provincial branch, English National Opera North. (This subsequently became Opera North and was based in Leeds, the city closest to Harewood House, the eighteenth-century Adam mansion that was the ancestral home of the Harewoods.) Harewood also took a keen, sympathetic interest in the music festival that Britten and Pears established at Aldeburgh as a venue for the productions of the English Opera Group.

At Aldeburgh Lord Harewood met and fell in love with the aspiring concert pianist Marion Stein. They married in 1949. She was the daughter of the Austrian musician and musicologist Erwin Stein, who had been a pupil and friend of Arnold Schoenberg. After the Anschluss, when the Nazis took power in Austria, the Stein family were among the many Jewish people who fled to London. Here Erwin Stein took up a post as editor for Britten's publisher, Boosey & Hawkes. The two men soon established a warm relationship, so much so that between 1949 and 1953 Britten and Pears took over a couple of rooms in the Stein home in Melbury Road, Kensington, to serve as their London base when they were away from Aldeburgh.

Through Marion Stein and an unexpected connection with her royal husband, Britten now had entry into court circles. In May 1953 the Harewoods gave a dinner party at their home in Orme Square, Bayswater, which was attended by the Queen and Prince Philip: Britten and Pears were also guests. It was the first of several encounters. The Harewoods also introduced Britten to more distant members of the Royal Family, descendants of the German princelings and aristocrats whose titles had lost their significance with the establishment of the Weimar republic in 1919. At Christmas 1954 Britten and Pears stayed with the lengthily titled Prince Ludwig of Hesse and the Rhine and his wife, Princess Margaret, at their country home near Darmstadt. Britten told Erwin Stein that

> it has all been so interesting, and full of new experiences and atmospheres
> – a world in every sense alien to us … It is a curious, circumscribed world,
> this international Royal clan – there were, for instance, seven princes to

the family dinner! Some are fascinating, Barbara of Prussia, and Francis of Bavaria, some dull or just effete. [152]

Entry into this marginalized, rarefied milieu is surely a contributing factor in Britten's increasing distance from common human experience that marked his life and art in his later years.

In March 1952 Britten was again on holiday with royalty, staying with the Harewoods at the Austrian ski resort of Gargellen before travelling on to Wiesbaden for the German premiere of *Billy Budd*. According to Lord Harewood it was during this holiday that the idea for the opera to follow *Billy Budd* was first broached. This was *Gloriana*, Britten's contribution to the coming Coronation festivities, which was to portray the difficult relationship between the ageing Queen Elizabeth I and her young, headstrong favourite, the Earl of Essex. It was a story that had been related by the Bloomsbury writer Lytton Strachey in his successful book *Elizabeth and Essex* (1928). Harewood had a special interest in the young Essex since he was a direct descendant of the Earl. When the opera was finally performed before the Queen as part of the Coronation celebrations, many critics took the view that this unhappy story of her aged ancestor was not an appropriate subject to put before the radiant young Queen on her Coronation day.

Britten was very much taken with Harewood's suggestion, but, always intent on advancing his role in the opera world, he stipulated that before he committed himself to the project, the opera should be formally declared to be part of the Coronation festivities, to be, as Lord Harewood remembered Britten insisting, 'made in some way official, not quite commanded but at least accepted as part of the celebrations'.[153] Harewood was also a cousin of Alan 'Tommy' Lascelles, who was the Queen's private secretary, and he arranged to meet him at Buckingham Palace to discuss the bestowing of the royal approval. This was duly obtained, together with an extra favour and mark of encouragement: the opera *Gloriana* was allowed to be dedicated 'by gracious permission to Her Majesty Queen Elizabeth II in honour of whose Coronation it was composed'.

Despite the many doubts and reservations of Peter Pears, Britten accepted the commission underwritten by the Royal Opera House. He then had to consider whom to approach to write the libretto. He decided on William Plomer, a South African friend of E.M. Forster with whom he had already worked on a couple of operas that had not come to completion. They quickly set to work in May 1952, having little more than a year in which to complete the text and the music. Britten felt he had to get to know the Elizabethan period better. He was grateful when Plomer sent him J.E. Neale's 1934 biography of the first Queen Elizabeth. From it, he told his librettist, 'I haven't yet felt the "corrective" to Strachey; but I am learning a lot about the extraordinary woman and time.'[154] Despite the close production deadline, as he started work Britten was clearly confident, excited and optimistic about the project. He went on, 'My feelings at the moment are that I want the opera to be crystal clear, with lovely pageantry ... but linked by a strong story about the Queen & Essex – strong & simple. A tall order, but I think we can do it!' Britten is now reaching into traditions in opera that he has not touched before. The very subject of the new work relates it to bel canto opera, and the inclusion of pageantry and also ballet give it the dance dimension that was long a feature of French opera and, in the days of grand opera in Paris in the nineteenth century, considered indispensable. As an opera composer Britten is now moving far beyond the stark simplicities of *Peter Grimes*.

As he began scoring *Gloriana* Britten also continued his research into its historical setting. His new aristocratic connections were a help. Lord Harewood arranged for him and Pears to visit Hatfield House, the house of the Marquess of Salisbury and his wife. Salisbury was a direct descendant of Sir Robert Cecil, chief minister and adviser to Queen Elizabeth I. In his letter of thanks to the Marchioness Britten acknowledged the great help the visit had been in his quest to assimilate period details: 'It was completely fascinating to see the wonderful house and the marvels it contains, and it was most kind of you and Lord Salisbury to take so much trouble & thought in showing it to us ... It is hard to exaggerate how inspiring these beautiful contemporary objects are.'[155] To recall that Britten is to some extent following in the footsteps of Donizetti, who in the 1820s and '30s wrote four operas on the subject of the Tudor period in England, and particularly of the first Queen Elizabeth, is to realize how much more both the words and the music of *Gloriana* are decked out with historical particulars of the time. There is a historical detailing in *Gloriana* that is not to be found in the Donizetti operas.

As the Coronation and the premiere of his new opera drew closer Britten had to show again that capacity for intense commitment and sheer hard work that was one of his many endowments as a composer. A commission for a new opera, which was to be *The Turn of the Screw*, lay unattended to. He complained anxiously 'I am seriously behindhand with my own commitments, many of which were postponed by Gloriana. Not least among them is my opera for Venice next year.'[156] In March 1953, some weeks after William Plomer had visited Aldeburgh to confer on the text of the opera, and almost three months to the day before the royal gala premiere at Covent Garden was to take place, Britten wrote to him, obviously in extreme haste, 'So sorry to have neglected you for so long ... I've been sitting at the score of Gloriana all day & almost every night since you left. She's well on the way to being finished now, & will be, I hope ...'[157]

His hopes were realized. The opera was completed on time and the premiere duly took place on 8 June 1953. It was a state and social occasion as much as the first performance of an opera. For Britten it was a catastrophe. He expressed his disappointment and disgust with that glittering and distinguished first night audience by resorting to a metaphor identical to the one employed by Elgar to describe the first public audience to hear his Second Symphony. Britten wrote that 'You didn't miss much on Monday night because the Gala was a shocking occasion – an audience of stuck pigs.'[158] Lord Harewood confirmed their sense of the extent of the failure of that first night; it was, he wrote, 'one of the great disasters of operatic history.'[159] The disappointing reception had to do with the composition of the audience, prominent people who were there at that royal occasion for reasons of social prestige: diplomats, bankers, socialites, politicians. William Plomer, who was not as distressed by the first night as Britten, confirmed this when he wrote to his brother that

> the audience was so largely official that it was afraid the stuffing might run out of its stuffed shirts, and was not as demonstrative as a musical audience. The Royal Family turned up in force and splendour, and I had some conversation with them in the 1st interval ... They seemed to enjoy themselves and said very nice things. [160]

The Queen was far from displeased with the opera. As an American journalist reported,

> Elizabeth II, unlike most of the others in the audience, obviously was not disturbed by the thought that Britten was violating the mood of the fairy-tale myth which was being woven around her and her Coronation. Having approved the score and script beforehand, she evidently preferred

a dramatic production of a tragedy built around some of the stark realities of her ancestor to fanciful nonsense about a New Elizabethan Age.[161]

Nevertheless two months after that gala night Britten was still feeling acutely the pain caused by the reception of *Gloriana*. To his loving and very supportive friend Elizabeth Mayer on Long Island he confided his deep upset at the opera's reception, particularly by the press: 'But – there is no point in glossing this fact over – we all feel so kicked around, so bewildered by the venom, that it is difficult to maintain one's balance.'[162] Nevertheless in the course of its first run *Gloriana* was increasingly well received by audiences and proved to be a financial success.

Today, going on seventy years after what Britten considered to be a painful debacle, *Gloriana* has an established position within the canon of Britten operas. It is far from being a minor work. But few would maintain that it ranks with the three great masterpieces: *Peter Grimes*, *Billy Budd* and *The Turn of the Screw*. However even as a work of secondary achievement it rightly enjoys occasional performances. It offers a pageant and some powerfully dramatic moments from the reign of Queen Elizabeth I, together with a good deal of pleasing, virtuosic music evoking the period. But it does not touch the profound, existential issues that Britten's three great operas engage with.

Britten completed *The Turn of the Screw*, the last of this historic trio of works, in 1954. He was to write several other operas after that time but none was to have the thematic and musical richness of these earlier, post-war works. For some twelve years, from his return from the United States in 1942 until the first performance of *The Turn of the Screw*, opera had been the form that was at the centre of Britten's musical ambitions and preoccupations. He composed a great variety of music during this dozen-year period but opera was his principal concern and his finest achievement – and not only as a composer but also as a busy and enterprising impresario.

At the end of this period of his career Britten felt exhausted. A little more than a year after the first London performance of *The Turn of the Screw* at Sadler's Wells he and Pears decided on an extended break. At the end of October 1955 they set off on a world tour that would last for some six months. They went to Amsterdam, Stuttgart, Geneva and Zurich, and thence to Salzburg and Vienna. From Austria they proceeded into the former Yugoslavia and gave concerts in Zagreb and Belgrade. They went on into Turkey and from Istanbul flew to Pakistan. After Karachi they went on to

India, with visits to Delhi, Agra and Calcutta. Then on to Singapore and thence to Sumatra. In Bandung Britten heard live Indonesian music for the first time. In Bali he listened to a great deal of gamelan. Then he and Pears proceeded to Singapore and Hong Kong and thence to Japan, where Britten and Pears attended performances of the Noh play *Sumidagawa* by Kanze Motomasa and heard the Gagaku orchestra perform at the Imperial Palace. After a visit to Sri Lanka they returned to India, staying in Madras and Bombay before flying back to Europe. This long period of travel, which brought so many new musical and theatrical influences, can be seen to mark the end of Britten's single-minded dedication to opera. Certainly after his return to Britain he would go on to write more operas but they were no longer the pre-eminent works in his output. They lack the power of the three great operas from the years of austerity in Britain and are but one group within a very wide range of very disparate compositions.

A Midsummer Night's Dream shows a turning away from high seriousness. More than any other of the later operas, those of the 1960s and '70s, it shows a clear-cut disengagement from a recognizable social historical reality. This will be the case, to a greater or lesser extent, with all these last operas. Britten's version of Shakespeare's comedy was again a quickly completed project. He proudly told a journalist that it took only 'seven months for everything including the score'. He added that, 'This is not up to the speed of Mozart or Verdi, but these days when the line of musical language is broken, it is much rarer.'[163] The opera was created to celebrate the re-opening in 1960 of the Jubilee Hall in Aldeburgh following a major refurbishment. The sets were rapidly supplied by John Piper and the orchestra was small. If Britten was aiming for a popular success with the minimum outlay, then he achieved his objective. The reception by the critics was for the most part very positive and within a year the opera was performed in Sweden, Scotland, Germany, Italy, Switzerland, Canada and Japan. And to this day the work continues to be given stagings around the world.

The appeal of the work is clear to see – and to hear. The distinctively coloured music works well with the time-honoured words to evoke a forest fairyland. Right from the outset the string glissandi give us the woodland hush and the movement of branches. Interestingly and illuminatingly, Paul Kildea has compared the woodland murmur in Britten's score with the works of the painter Richard Dadd, 'the Victorian murderer, Bedlam inmate and fantastic artist whose evocative paintings depict the dangerous and alluring world of fairies and the supernatural'.[164] But the delicate world of faery also has to contain within it the stumbling and galumphing around of the rude mechanicals as they go about rehearsing their dramatization of the story of Pyramus and Thisbe. Britten's music entertainingly exploits the comic situation. Pyramus at times launches into blaring heroics that recall and gently satirize Verdi. And in Thisbe's mad scene there is more overt satire, this time of Donizetti's *Lucia di Lammermoor*. The mad scene, which is one of the most famous scenes in opera, was one of Britten's great dislikes. Ever the keen student of opera, he attended the revival of this work at Covent Garden in February 1959 when Joan Sutherland sang the title role. He reported to Peter Pears that 'it was the most horrid experience. It is the most awful work; common & vulgar, very boring, no subtleties, poor tunes (the old Sextet is the best – Donald Duck and Clara Cluck), just as if Mozart, Gluck & all (written in 1835) hadn't existed.' Nor was he particularly impressed by Joan Sutherland, who, after seven years as a 'house soprano' at Covent Garden, was establishing herself as a star in the larger world of opera: 'she sang it well, it suits her perfectly, but to my taste with no real musicality or warmth – she'd been taught the Italian style like a dog is taught tricks.'[165]

Britten was disconcerted to find that he was virtually alone in his depreciation of what time has shown to have been a historic performance of the Donizetti opera. Very much the opera impresario, he was always attentive to the responses and moods of audiences. After his success with *A Midsummer Night's Dream* he turned in his next 1960s opera to the medium of television, which in the twenty years and more since the premiere of *Peter Grimes* had grown exponentially in audience and popularity.

In November 1967, following the success of a 1966 BBC studio production of *Billy Budd* under Charles Mackerras, Britten entered into discussion with BBC Television about the possibility of creating a broadcast opera based on the Henry James ghost story *Owen Wingrave*. Eventually the Corporation decided to commission the project for the sum of £10,000, a sizeable amount for such a programme at that time. Britten invited Myfanwy Piper to prepare a libretto and early in 1968 she began the first sketches. Henry James had seen the dramatic potential of his novella and had adapted it as a play, but like George Bernard Shaw many years before, Britten and his librettist found James's playscript inadequate. Piper set about providing an altogether new one, but not with altogether successful results.

The television opera explores the conflict between the entrenched traditions of the Wingraves, an ancient and distinguished military family residing in their grand mansion Paramore, and the sudden realization by the youngest member of the family, the idealistic Owen Wingrave, that militarism and war are barbaric and that peace is the noblest of human aspirations. In places in the opera, the peace aria for instance, the work sounds like a proclamation of Britten's pacifist beliefs. When Owen's family members learn of his conversion to pacifism, they turn violently against him. His grandfather disinherits him and his fiancée questions his courage and humiliates him. She challenges him to sleep in the room in Paramore in which, according to family legend, earlier Wingraves had died when their bravery had been doubted. Owen readily accepts the challenge and is subsequently found dead in the room.

The two conflicting views of human life have been well enough articulated in the piece. But this conclusion can only come across as abrupt. It is an unsuccessful denouement both narratively and musically. Compared with the profound and layered investigation of violence and war in *Billy Budd*, that in *Owen Wingrave* can only seem schematic and underdeveloped.

The opera was filmed at the concert venue that Britten and Pears had created at Snape Maltings, near Aldeburgh, and broadcast on BBC Television on 16 May 1971. The horrors of the war in Vietnam, as relayed day after day by television news, were very much in the public mind. The Campaign for Nuclear Disarmament, of which Britten was a long-time member, was conspicuously active. And pacifism, very much an emphasis within the counterculture, became a theme of mainstream entertainment and culture: 'Make Love, Not War!' was a familiar slogan in the late 1960s and early '70s, and the mantra of John Lennon and Yoko Ono, 'All we are saying is give peace a chance', had a similar popular currency.

Although Britten's television opera conformed and catered to the progressive spirit of the time, it was not especially successful. Britten himself was not comfortable with the medium of television. He disliked the actual filming, 'this rough and tumble at the Maltings', and the filmed production was stilted and cramped. But the worst failing was that Britten was not thinking or expressing himself operatically. He virtually said as much when he told the *Guardian*'s music critic Edward Greenfield that 'I don't feel that Owen Wingrave is a "grand opera" ... For one thing there is no chorus (except a small off-stage one), the orchestra is fairly small, and there are comparatively few protagonists, and the point of the work is reasoned intimate discussion or soliloquies.'[166]

The last five words suggest how Britten's sense of opera has narrowed and shrunk compared with that shown in *Peter Grimes* or *Billy Budd* of around two decades earlier. Discussion and soliloquies are not enough to sustain an opera. Britten's last opera, *Death in Venice*, plays out in an even more circumscribed space. It is a setting of Thomas Mann's novella and a good deal of the opera is an expression of the stream of consciousness of the central character, the writer Gustav von Aschenbach. At the outset, in Munich, he ponders his painful loss of creativity. He is persuaded to undertake a visit to his beloved Venice as a possible cure. Upon arrival in La Serenissima he finds himself in a hotel on the Lido where he becomes fascinated by Tadzio, a young and attractive Polish boy who is staying there with his family. Aschenbach, to his great torment, becomes ever more obsessed with this figure of beauty. He craves contact with him, pursues him and even stays on in Venice when cholera strikes the city and other foreign visitors hurry away. Aschenbach cannot stand to lose sight of Tadzio. The boy only responds to his gaze when the writer is dying: it is Tadzio, so it seems, who conducts the ageing author from this world into the next at the end of the opera.

Tadzio is not a singing part. He and his family and friends express themselves through body language and movement rather than song. The dance elements in the opera were created by the highly experienced choreographer Frederick Ashton. Myfanwy Piper was again Britten's librettist, but Peter Pears was also involved in some of the literary decisions. Britten was keenly aware that *Death in Venice* was 'probably Peter's last major operatic part'. He told Schuyler Chapin, General Manager of the Metropolitan Opera, after the success of the opera in New York, that 'The part was of course written with his personality and voice in mind, but a really great artist gives much more to a part than is already there.'[167] And it is moving testimony to his love for his partner that he deferred the heart surgery that was essential to his own well-being in order to complete this last opera for Peter Pears. At the end of 1974 he told a journalist from *The Times* that 'I wanted passionately to finish this piece before anything happened. I had to keep going and then, when I had finished, put myself into the doctor's hands.'

One dramaturgical device that Britten and Pears decided on together was the continuing metamorphosis of the hotel manager into a series of other characters, each of which is an ominous representation of death. He is earlier the traveller who lures Aschenbach to the decadence of Venice rather than to his summer house in the healthy air of the Alps. He is the elderly fop, giggling in his make-up, who indicates and suggests an interest in Italian rough trade. He is the gondolier who insists on taking Aschenbach to the fateful Lido against his will and then abruptly and mysteriously disappears. He is the hotel barber who dyes the ageing writer's hair to make him appear younger and more attractive. (This is but one in a succession of indignities that Aschenbach undergoes as his obsession with Tadzio takes hold of him.) The mutant character then turns into the Leader of the Players in the *commedia dell'arte* troupe that visits the hotel, enacting the crudities of life that contrast with the ethereal drift towards death that now carries Aschenbach along. The same character also becomes the Dionysian figure who is the victor over Apollo in Aschenbach's humiliating death vision.

Aschenbach's story is bedecked with mythological allusions, including these to Apollo and Dionysus. Perhaps clogged is a better word, because they certainly weaken the dramatic trenchancy of the opera, and perhaps even make it at times seem pretentious. In his play *The Habit of Art*, which describes a supposed meeting late in life between Britten and his old friend W.H. Auden, Alan Bennett has the Auden character voice some outspoken criticism of this opera. He declares

> I can't write a furtive libretto. You like boys, Ben. No amount of dressing Tadzio up as a vision of Apollo can alter the fact that Dionysus for you comes in a grey flannel suit or cricket whites. This is an old man lusting after a boy and Apollo has got fuck all to do with it.[168]

The insistence on mythological significance certainly weighs the opera down, as do some of the lengthy balletic elements: the Olympian athlete games danced by boys and the extended *commedia dell'arte*. These elements are surely introduced to give us the sense of a wider world, one beyond that of the individual, tortured consciousness of Aschenbach. Opera is not cantata and requires the establishment of a social, that is to say more than a lyrical, reality and of the conflicts that are the inherent constituents of such a reality.

Certainly there are some fine things in Britten's last opera. There is a compelling power to the recitatives, inspired perhaps by those in the *St Matthew Passion* of Heinrich Schütz, which Peter Pears greatly enjoyed performing around the time Britten was engaged in the composition of the opera. There is the memorable dream sequence of Dionysian rout with the cacophonous beating of drums and cymbals and the primitive cries of the singers. And then, in contrast, the moving orchestral finale as Tadzio, at the very last, comes to him, not in life but in death.

For all its tacit claims to profundity and its extended production numbers, however, *Death in Venice* lacks the musical and literary conflict, the sheer drama that makes for a successful opera. As we listen to the final, very moving strains that mark the ending of Britten's many years in the opera house, we cannot but conclude that his greatest achievements in the genre lay years behind him. More specifically they ended in the mid-1950s, when *The Turn of the Screw* had its premiere. This work, along with *Peter Grimes* and *Billy Budd*, goes to make up a trio of achievement that is historic, not just for opera in Britain but in the North Atlantic world as a whole. The contrast between *Death in Venice* and *The Turn of the Screw* is clear and very illuminating about the nature of the genre. To Desmond Shawe-Taylor, who wrote to him about the latter work, Britten insisted that

> It *does* work as an opera I feel, & I think in many ways you are right about the subject matter being, as it were, nearest to me of any I have yet chosen (although what that indicates of my own character I shouldn't like to say!) … But it *must* be an opera in its own right, & must stand or fall by that.[169]

This closeness to Britten's deepest personal concerns is what gives *The Turn of the Screw* a thematic directness and a dramatic suspense lacking in the revisiting of the same issues of experience nearly two decades later in *Death in Venice*. The deepest thematic level in *The Turn of the Screw* has to do with the exploitation and corruption of innocence. What would have been especially shocking to audiences in the 1950s was that it involved the corruption of two young children, Miles and Flora, by a former valet in the household, Peter Quint. Clearly there are hints of paedophilia, possibly of a homosexual kind (whether in verbal terms or in actual sexual activity is left intriguingly unspecified). Biographers suggest that young boys were often a temptation and a reputational danger for Benjamin Britten. His interest in David Hemmings, the first boy to sing the part of Miles, and who later became a star in films such as Antonioni's *Blow-Up* (1966), was judged by Peter Pears to be almost catastrophic.[170]

The composer's keen engagement is unmissable in the music of *The Turn of the Screw*, especially in the variegated musical interludes, each of which is a variation on the twelve-note theme established at the beginning of the first act. The libretto is at times less effective, the words given to Peter Quint and his lover Miss Jessel being at times overblown. Nevertheless the narrative moves along swiftly and very engagingly. The story unfolds in a grand country estate, Bly, such as has often served as an important centre in English cultural history and has also been a setting in some of the greatest English novels from Jane Austen's *Pride and Prejudice* to D.H. Lawrence's *Women in Love*. But at Bly there is no longer the sustaining and welcoming stability of the past. The landowner is a perpetual absentee, completely indifferent to the house and to the children who are his relatives. Interested only in his busy life in London (brilliantly and succinctly conveyed by the music), he urgently discourages the young Governess he has engaged, from contacting him about anything to do with life at Bly. *The Turn of the Screw* is about the ending of vital, healthy English country house culture and its descent into decadence. Again perhaps only an English-speaking outsider, an American novelist such as Henry James, could intimate the deeper decadence and abuse that lay at the heart of this very English story.

Scarcely has the Governess arrived at Bly than she is confronted with the news that the seemingly angelic Miles has been strictly forbidden to return to his boarding school. Mrs Grose, the housekeeper, and the voice of homely common sense in the opera, attempts to reassure the governess that, though Miles may be naughty at times, he is not bad. But then comes another shock when the Governess, strolling in the garden, sees a sinister-looking man looking out from the tower and then again, more intimidatingly, through the hall window. The housekeeper observes that the ghostly figure looks like Peter Quint, now dead, who had been valet to the departed owner of Bly. He had exploited his trust, she explains, by being 'very free' with Miss Jessel, the previous governess. Quint had also been 'free with' the children, in particular with Miles. The music of malaise that pervades the opera is intensified when at night Quint is heard calling to Miles and he is joined by Miss Jessel calling eerily to Flora from across the lake.

In the second act the Governess is further shocked when Miles speaks with unambiguous explicitness of 'the others'. Her psychological stability is still more shaken when she enters the schoolroom to see the ghost of Miss Jessel weeping at the memory of how Peter Quint had reduced her and then finally ruined her. Horrified by the thought of being responsible for the two children in this haunted, infected and infecting mansion, the Governess decides with tortured reluctance to break her agreement with the children's guardian and to write to him about conditions at Bly. Quint, however, induces Miles to steal the letter she writes. Mrs Grose resolves to take Flora away from Bly: for this level-headed woman the presence of evil spirits is no illusion. But the Governess will not accept defeat and stays on at Bly, insisting on questioning Miles about the malign influence that corrupted him when it was a living being and still continues to influence him as a ghost. The Governess insists that Miles tell her who is seeking to manipulate him from the beyond. Quint's voice interrupts hers. The two of them compete for Miles's loyalty. Strain and tension mount in the concluding exchanges. The opera ends with a moment of powerful and chilling drama as a tormented Miles cries out the four words, 'Peter Quint, you devil', and falls dead in the arms of the Governess.

The Turn of the Screw employs much smaller operatic devices than *Death in Venice*. In this 1950s composition there are no great ensemble moments and no ballet, and yet this earlier work is far more powerful and piercing in its effect. Though not endowed with the multitude of cultural references that pervade the later work, *The Turn of the Screw* is far more profound and challenging in its multiplicity of nuanced and deeply disturbing implications. The Britten operas that follow *The Turn of the Screw* contain music of distinction, but none of them achieve a finely realized operatic art and expression, *dramma per musica*, to compare with the great trio of *Peter Grimes*, *Billy Budd* and *The Turn of the Screw*. The fifteen years that saw their creation constitute one of the high points of the history of music in England, one that, it is worth insisting, was the greatest period of English opera since the time of Purcell.

Apart from the mysterious, ultimately undefinable force that we call genius, great works derive from the psychological and sociological context of their creator. It seems likely that the success of Britten's three greatest operas derives from his awareness of the profoundly variant position in which he found himself in English society in those years. He was a homosexual and a dedicated pacifist at a time when male warrior virtues were demanded and esteemed. From outsider status, which was undoubtedly painful, came the three masterpieces. They each offer a detailed sounding of the relationship between sensitive, well-intentioned individuals and societies that cannot comprehend them. In the two terrible wars that affected the western world for the greater part of the first half of the twentieth century, regimentation became the characteristic of western societies. The most memorable works of art that followed the ending of the Second World War are about the rejection of the norms of such regimentation. Francis Bacon's *Three Studies for Figures at the Base of a Crucifixion*, Orwell's *Nineteen Eighty-Four* and *The Outsider* of Albert Camus all share a concern with the fate of the individual alienated from the imposed norms of perception and behaviour. And this is true for Peter Grimes, Billy Budd and the Governess.

As British society in the 1950s moved away from the practical and emotional austerities demanded by wars and their aftermath, so did Britten's art. In the last twenty years of his life he became less the outsider and more an honoured figure, indeed a national treasure. His altered social and psychological situation inevitably led to a change of genre in his music. In his last two decades, indeed until the very end of his life, he continued to be a very productive composer, but it is no longer the music that evokes a social milieu or community such as we find in grand opera. After *The Turn of the Screw* Britten's finest music is inward-looking, lyrical, autobiographical. In his very last years the great opera composer turned to the symphony, the genre that the leading composers of the twentieth century – and especially Britten's two most important English predecessors, Elgar and Vaughan Williams – had resorted to as first choice in investigating and recording the impact upon them of the singular horrors of their time.

In the twentieth century the symphony became, as for the most part it had been at least since the time of Beethoven's *Eroica*, essentially a personal, autobiographical statement from the composer. This musical genre offered the widest, most detailed and most coloured medium for giving an account of the sequences of personal experience. This was more so by far even than the various types of chamber music, which could also be highly autobiographical, Britten's Third String Quartet, his last, being a most impressive instance.

An interesting rounding off of the story of the near eighty years of achievement created by Elgar, Vaughan Williams and Britten is that towards the end of his life Britten should begin writing 'A Sea Symphony', the very subject and title with which Vaughan Williams had begun his symphonic career back in 1910. (As part of his preparation Britten even arranged for a performance at the Aldeburgh Festival of *A Sea Symphony* by the composer whose music he had once so vehemently and regularly deplored.) Britten's notes for this undeveloped project suggest that his symphonic vision of the sea would have been very different from the Whitmanesque vistas scored by Vaughan Williams. The poems he had in mind for his sung symphony included ones by Herman Melville and Milton, Matthew Arnold's 'Dover Beach' and Shelley's 'Dirge'.[171] The proposed titles suggest that Britten's 'Sea Symphony' would have a very dark side. It would perhaps have taken cognisance of the horrors and sufferings of the later twentieth century of which Vaughan Williams in 1910 could not have been aware.

But Benjamin Britten, in his last symphony, certainly was. This was his Cello Symphony composed in 1963, the year of the assassination of President John F. Kennedy and at the height of the Cold War. It was written in association with the great Soviet cellist Mstislav Rostropovich and dedicated to him. The first performance was given in Moscow in March 1964 by the Moscow Philharmonic Orchestra. One of the contingent facts about this powerful work is that in it and through it Britten and his art managed to transcend the always dangerous and at times near catastrophic conflicts of the Cold War.

The work, however, does not ignore them, rather it renders them together with their potential for horror. Written during the year after the Cuban Missile Crisis, which came close to plunging the planet into nuclear war, the symphony has an undertow of danger, violence and menace. At times the effect of the music is to alarm, perhaps even to strike fear. The swell of hopeful feeling that surges up in the final bars of the last movement contains within its instrumentation that which undercuts and compromises the hope. The passage can be seen to be very much 'tacked on', more a quick rhetorical gesture than felt hope.

More characteristic and pervasive throughout this symphony are the sombre, clashing, deeply disturbing sounds led by the grinding cello at the beginning of the first movement. Then come the dramatic drums of war, shrills of pain and the failure of the, by now soothing, cello to console. The disturbing soundscape fades from our hearing into eerie lamentation. In the second movement, Presto inquieto, there is a would-be brightening, a quickening, an eddying in the strings. There is a lyrical moment of some beauty, but it is brief in what is overall a very short movement of brio feeling. The opening energy becomes febrile and scurries away into a nervy ghostliness.

The first movement of the symphony had occasionally allowed us to hear amidst all the tumult the still small voice of the individual in a way that reminds us of the symphonies of another of Britten's Soviet friends, Dmitri Shostakovich. But the long third movement, the Adagio, the heart of this piece, does not allow even this. Throughout it is bleak and intimidating. It begins with a harsh, long drawn-out passage that suggests both war and a funeral march. There follows a passionate lament from the cello and then ghostly mournfulness from the woodwind. The Russian audience at the first performance can have had little doubt about Britten's acute understanding of their sufferings in recent times. After the lamentation there comes again, with a crash, the violence first rendered in the opening movement. All that is left for the cellist's cadenza is a long, painful elegy.

Without a break Britten takes us into the fourth and final movement marked Passacaglia: Andante allegro. There is a sudden determination to alleviate matters, to brighten the music. A trumpet attempts to be cheerful, but within a very few bars a sardonic note enters. There continues to be an ambiguity to the seemingly revived spirits and, as I have suggested, the swelling hope at the very end does not long endure or convince. Is this rhetoric or belief? It is a similar question to the one posed at the end of the Fifth Symphony of Shostakovich. The evidence of the first ninety per cent and more of Britten's symphony must surely imply the former.

In the midst of the Cold War this powerful, passionate symphony, brought to the Soviet capital from the West, must have offered its audience a keen and unsentimental understanding of the violence and suffering with which they were all too familiar. The lasting implication of this great work, so very much a product of the twentieth century, is the need to specify and acknowledge the horrors of time past, and for those on both sides of the Iron Curtain to go beyond them. The Cello Symphony is a work that offers difficult, painful understanding. It also offers greeting – from the West to the East. It is a memorable response to human enormities.

At the turn of the century Edward Elgar had been able to show that England was a land that could produce music that spoke profoundly to the human mind and feelings. Some three quarters of a century later Benjamin Britten, following in the musical culture that Elgar had revived, created a music that spoke not just of and to England but also, as German music had done throughout the nineteenth century, to a larger world. Elgar made English music again resound. By the time of Benjamin Britten's Cello Symphony that music had an international resonance.

References

1 Keith Alldritt, *Churchill the Writer: His Life as a Man of Letters* (Hutchinson, 1992) pp. 19–22.

2 Quoted in Jerrold Northrop Moore, *Edward Elgar: A Creative Life* (Oxford University Press, 1984), p. 247.

3 *Birmingham Daily Mail*, 15 October 1903.

4 W.C. Stockley, *Fifty Years of Music in Birmingham: Being the Reminiscences of W.C. Stockley from 1850 to 1900* (Hudson and Son, 1913), pp. 34–5.

5 Jerrold Northrop Moore (ed.), *Elgar: Letters of a Lifetime* (Oxford University Press, 1990), p. 9.

6 Ibid., p. 15.

7 Ibid., p. 23.

8 Ibid., p. 56.

9 Ibid., p. 67.

10 Ibid., p. 76.

11 Ibid., p. 298.

12 Michael Kennedy, *Portrait of Elgar* (Oxford University Press, 1968), p. 90.

13 Jerrold Northrop Moore, *Edward Elgar, A Creative Life* (Oxford University Press, 1984), p. 33.

14 Kennedy, *Portrait of Elgar*, p. 91.

15 In an interview with Jules Huret, Mallarmé defined his understanding of the word 'symbol': 'C'est le parfait usage de mystère qui constitue le symbole: évoquer petit à petit un objet pour montrer un état d'âme, ou, inversement, choisir un objet et en dégager un état d'âme, par une série de déchiffrements.' Stéphane Mallarmé, 'Réponses à des enquêtes sur l'évolution littéraire', *Oeuvres Complètes* (Gallimard, 1945), p. 869.

16 Kennedy, *Portrait of Elgar*, p. 108.

17 Moore (ed.), *Elgar: Letters of a Lifetime*, p. 87.

18   Percy M. Young (ed.), *Edward Elgar: A Future for English Music and Other Lectures* (Dobson Books, 1968), p. 29.

19   Ibid., p. 45.

20   Ibid., p. 55.

21   Ibid., p. 93.

22   Ibid., pp. 132–3.

23   Ibid., p. 143.

24   Ibid., p. 165.

25   Ibid., p. 187.

26   Ibid., p. 155.

27   Ibid., p. 28.

28   Ibid., p. 223.

29   Moore (ed.), *Elgar: Letters of a Lifetime*, p. 505.

30   *Birmingham Daily Post*, 22 March 1907.

31   Moore (ed.), *Elgar: Letters of a Lifetime*, p. 773.

32   W.H. Reed, *Elgar As I Knew Him* (Oxford University Press, 1936), pp. 68–9.

33   Michael Kennedy, *The Works of Ralph Vaughan Williams* (Oxford University Press, 1980), p. 610.

34   Ibid., p. 195.

35   *Strand Magazine* (May 1904), p. 544.

36   Mrs Richard Powell, *Edward Elgar: Memories of a Variation* (Methuen, 1949), p. 104.

37   Ibid., p. 107.

38   Ibid., pp. 79–80.

39   From a letter by Elgar, 'The Vernal Anemones', *The Times*, 28 April 1923.

40   Jerrold Northrop Moore (ed.), *Edward Elgar: The Windflower Letters* (Oxford University Press, 1989), p. 83.

41   Ibid., p. 604.

42   Ibid., p. 603.

43   Ibid., p. 598.

44   Ibid., p. 609.

45   W.H. Read, *Elgar* (Dent, 1939), p. 105.

46   Kennedy, *Works of Ralph Vaughan Williams*, p. 234.

47   Moore (ed), *Edward Elgar: The Windflower Letters*, p. 329.

48   Kennedy, *Works of Ralph Vaughan Williams*, p. 263.

49   Ibid., p. 785.

50   Theodor W. Adorno, 'Music Language and Composition' in *Essays in Music* (University of California Press, 2002), p. 122.

51   J.H. Plumb, *The Collected Essays, vol. xi: The Making of a Historian* (Harvester, 1988) p. 190.

52   Kennedy, *Works of Ralph Vaughan Williams*, p. 100.

53   D.H. Lawrence, 'Whitman', in *Studies in Classic American Literature* (Penguin, 1971), p. 179.

54   Ibid., p. 181.

55   Alain Frogley, 'History and Geography: The Early Orchestral Works and the First Three Symphonies', in *The Cambridge Companion to Vaughan Williams*, ed. Alain Frogley and Aidan J. Thomson (Cambridge University Press, 2013), p. 9.

56   Hugh Cobbe (ed.), *Letters of Ralph Vaughan Williams, 1895–1958* (Oxford University Press, 2008), p. 74.

57   Kennedy, *Works of Ralph Vaughan Williams*, p. 127.

58   David Manning (ed.), *Vaughan Williams on Music* (Oxford University Press, 2008), p. 41.

59   Ibid., p. 40.

60   Cobbe, *Letters of Ralph Vaughan Williams*, p. 93.

61   For an account of Vaughan Williams's reluctant support for the Boer War, see Keith Alldritt, *Vaughan Williams, Composer, Radical, Patriot* (Robert Hale, 2015), pp. 94–5

62   The first published score, dating from 1920, was recorded by the BBC Symphony Orchestra under Martyn Brabbins and issued by Hyperion Records in 2017.

63   Arnold Bax, *Farewell My Youth* (Longmans, 1943), p. 93.

64   Quoted in Ursula Vaughan Williams, *RVW: A Biography of Ralph Vaughan Williams* (Oxford University Press, 1988), p. 129.

65   Cobbe, *Letters of Ralph Vaughan Williams*, p. 109.

66   Ibid., p. 265.

67   Ursula Vaughan Williams, *RVW*, p. 140.

68   Ibid., p. 142.

69   Kennedy, *Works of Ralph Vaughan Williams*, p. 203.

70   Ibid., p. 202.

71   Cobbe, *Letters of Ralph Vaughan Williams*, p. 231.

72   British Library MS Music 1714/1/9/98

73   Cobbe, *Letters of Ralph Vaughan Williams*, p.255

74   Letter from Arthur Benjamin, 21 April 1935. British Library, MS Music 1714/1/9/113.

75   British Library, MS Music 1714/1/9/126.

76   The story of this love affair is related in Alldritt, *Vaughan Williams, Composer, Radical, Patriot*, pp. 243–73 and in Janet Tennant, *Mistress and Music: the second Mrs Vaughan Williams* (Albion Music Limited, 2017), pp.80 et seq.

77   Cobbe, *Letters of Ralph Vaughan Williams*, p. 359.

78   Ibid., p. 360.

79   Ursula Vaughan Williams, *RVW*, p. 254.

80   Kennedy, *Works of Ralph Vaughan Williams*, p. 301.

81   Ibid., p. 303.

82   Ibid., p. 302.

83   Ibid., p. 349.

84   Peter Maxwell Davies, quoted in *The Cambridge Companion to Vaughan Williams*, ed. Frogley and Thomson, p. 302.

85   Byron Adams, 'The Stages of Revision of Vaughan Williams's Sixth Symphony', Musical Quarterly, lxxiii/3 (1989), pp. 382–400; repr. in *Vaughan Williams Essays*, ed. Byron Adams and Robin Wells (Ashgate, 2003), pp. 1–16.

86   Wilfrid Mellers, *Vaughan Williams and the Vision of Albion*, 2nd edn (Barrie and Jenkins, 1991), p. 194.

87   Cobbe, *Letters of Ralph Vaughan Williams*, p. 499.

88   British Library, MS Music 1714/1/22/112.

89   Alldritt, *Vaughan Williams, Composer, Radical, Patriot*, p. 235.

90   Kennedy, *Works of Ralph Vaughan Williams*, p. 343.

91   Alain Frogley, *Vaughan Williams's Ninth Symphony* (Oxford University Press, 2001), p. 73.

92   Mellers, *Vaughan Williams and the Vision of Albion*, p. 236.

93   Cobbe, *Letters of Ralph Vaughan Williams*, p. 618.

94   Ibid., p. 627.

95   Manning, *Vaughan Williams on Music*, p. 627.

96   John Evans (ed.), *Journeying Boy: The Diaries of the Young Benjamin Britten, 1928–1938* (Faber and Faber, 2009), p. 276.

97   Ibid., p. 135.

98   Ibid., p. 249.

99   Ibid., p. 278.

100 Ibid., p. 361.

101 Ibid., p. 273.

102 Ibid., p. 292.

103 W.H. Auden, 'Rilke in English', *New Republic* (6 September 1939), p. 135.

104 The German line is 'und die findigen Tiere merken es schon / dass wir nicht sehr verlässlich zu Haus sind / in der gedeuteten Welt.'

105 Donald Mitchell, *Britten and Auden in the Thirties: The Year 1936* (Faber and Faber, 1981), p. 38.

106 Evans, *Journeying Boy*, p. 374.

107 Ibid., p. 375.

108 Edmund Wilson, *Shores of Light* (Doubleday, 1952), p. 669.

109 Nigel Nicolson (ed.), *The Letters of Virginia Woolf*, vol. vi (Chatto and Windus, 1980), p. 318.

110 John Maynard Keynes, *The Collected Writings of John Maynard Keynes*, vol. xxviii: Social, Political and Literary Writings (The Royal Economic Society, 1982), p. 128.

111 Donald Mitchell, Philip Reed and Mervyn Cooke (eds), *Letters from a Life: Selected Letters and Diaries of Benjamin Britten, 1913–1976*, 6 vols (i–iii: Faber and Faber; iv–vi: Boydell Press, 1991–2012), i, p. 502.

112 John Bridcut, *Britten's Children* (Faber and Faber, 2006), p. 75.

113 Mitchell, Reed and Cooke, *Letters from a Life*, i, pp. 983–4.

114 Ibid., p. 992.

115 BBC Radio, 11 August 1965.

116 Paul Kildea, *Benjamin Britten: A Life in the Twentieth Century* (Allen Lane, 2013), p. 179.

117 Donald Mitchell and John Evans (eds), *Benjamin Britten: Pictures from a Life, 1913–1976* (Faber and Faber, 1978), pl. 113.

118 Ian Bostridge, booklet notes to his recording of Les Illuminations with Simon Rattle and the Berlin Philharmonic, EMI Classics, 2005, p. 6.

119 Ibid., p. 5.

120 Author's translation. The French original reads: 'Ce sont des villes! C'est un peuple pour qui sont montés ces Alleghanys et ces Libans de rêve! Des chalets de cristal et de bois se meuvent sur des rails et des poulies invisibles. Les vieux cratères ceints de colosses et de palmiers de cuivre régissent mélodieusement dans les feux [...] Des cortèges de Mabs en robes rousses, opalines, montent des ravines. Là-haut, les pieds dans la cascade et les ronces, les cerfs tettent Diane. Les Bacchantes des banlieues sanglotent et la lune brûle et hurle. Vénus entre dans les cavernes des forgerons et des ermites [...] Des groupes de beffrois chantent les idées des peuples. Des châteaux bâtis en os sont la musique inconnue.'

121 Mitchell, Reed and Cooke, *Letters from a Life*, ii, pp. 799–800.

122 Ibid., p. 881.

123 Howard Pollack, *Aaron Copland: The Life and Work of an Uncommon Man* (Faber and Faber, 2000), p. 75.

124 Mitchell, Reed and Cooke, *Letters from a Life*, ii, p. 1013.

125 Ibid., p. 1037.

126 Ibid., p. 1059.

127 In August 1944 Britten was reading Pound, who he considered 'a very remarkable poet'. Learning of Pound's arrest in Italy by American soldiers on charges of treasonable material in his broadcasts from Rome, Britten asked Pound's friend Ronald Duncan 'can't anything be done about helping Pound – he's obviously a great man, and we haven't so many that we can go around spilling their blood'. Ibid., p. 1222.

128 Ibid., p. 1089.

129 Ibid., pp. 1123–4.

130 Ibid., p. 1130.

131 Ibid., p. 1173.

132 Ibid., p. 1162.

133 Ibid., p. 1216.

134 Ibid., p. 1216.

135 Ibid., p. 1182.

136 Ibid., p. 1219.

137 Ibid., p. 1243.

138 Ibid., p. 1243.

139 *The Times*, 1 June 1985.

140 Mitchell, Reed and Cooke, *Letters from a Life*, ii, p. 1268.

141 Ibid., iii, p. 681.

142 Ibid., ii, p. 1285

143 John Adams, *Hallelujah Junction: Composing an American Life* (Faber and Faber, 2008), p. 223.

144 Mitchell, Reed and Cooke, *Letters from a Life*, iii, p. 251.

145 Ibid., p. 242.

146 Ibid., pp. 198–9.

147 Ibid., p. 393.

148 Ibid., p. 506.

149 Ibid., pp. 500–501.

150 Ibid., p. 503.

151 Ibid., p. 535.

152 Ibid., iv, p. 199.

153 Lord Harewood, *The Tongues and the Bones* (Weidenfeld and Nicolson, 1981), p. 137.

154 Mitchell, Reed and Cooke, *Letters from a Life*, iv, p. 63.

155 Ibid., p. 87.

156 Ibid., p. 137.

157 Ibid., p. 135.

158 Ibid., p. 147.

159 Harewood, *The Tongues and the Bones*, p. 138.

160 Quoted in Mitchell, Reed and Cooke, *Letters from a Life*, iv, p. 147.

161 Joseph Newman, *New York Herald Tribune*, 14 June 1953.

162 Mitchell, Reed and Cooke, *Letters from a Life*, iv, p. 177.

163 Benjamin Britten, 'A New Britten Opera', *Observer*, 5 June 1960.

164 Kildea, *A Life in the Twentieth Century*, p. 228.

165 Mitchell, Reed and Cooke, *Letters from a Life*, v, p. 119.

166 Ibid., vi, p. 412.

167 Ibid., p. 642.

168 Alan Bennett, *The Habit of Art* (Faber and Faber, 2010), p. 67.

169 Mitchell, Reed and Cooke, *Letters from a Life*, iv, p. 300.

170 Humphrey Carpenter, *Benjamin Britten: A Biography* (Faber and Faber, 1992), p. 357.

171 Mitchell, Reed and Cooke, *Letters from a Life*, v, p. 226.

Index